Play Together, Stay Together

Happy and Healthy Play Between People and Dogs

Karen B. London
Patricia B. McConnell

For information, contact:
McConnell Publishing, Ltd.
P.O. Box 447
Black Earth, WI 53515
(608) 767-2435
www.patriciamcconnell.com
Cover design by Julie Mueller, jam graphics & design
Printed in the United States of America

2 3 4 5 6 7 8 9

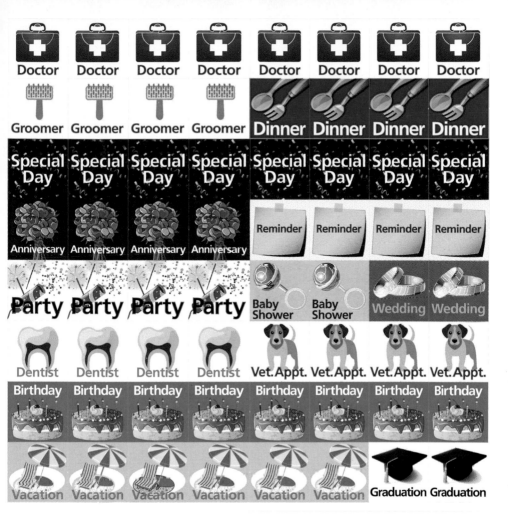

To Help You Remember...

All year long, your generous support of the important programs and activities of The HSUS is working to end cruelty, neglect and the exploitation of animals. It's a commitment to protecting all animals that we know you share with us.

Please use these convenient stickers to help you remember birthdays, anniversaries, veterinary appointments and other special dates. Simply peel off and affix a reminder to the special date.

We also hope you will complete the Emergency Phone Numbers and affix to a location next to your phone.

EMERGENCY PHONE NUMBERS

Police, Fire/Rescue: _____

Poison Control: _____

Physician: _____

Dentist: _____

Veterinarian: _____

Emergency Pet Clinic: _____

Local Animal Shelter: _____

Other: _____

Other: _____

Other: _____

The Humane Society of the United States
1255 23rd Street, NW, Suite 450 • Washington, DC 20037 • *humanesociety.org*

7 STEPS TO A HAPPIER PET

The Humane Society of the United States, in its constant battle to end animal neglect, cruelty and abuse, encourages all its members to take the following actions in support of animals.

- Have a heart, be smart and make sure your pet is spayed or neutered.
- Make sure your pet wears a collar and current identification tag, and consider having your pet microchipped to enable him to be returned to you if he loses his collar.
- To prevent animal behavioral problems, make sure you enroll your new puppy or dog in behavioral training classes.
- Animal behavioral problems can be health-related. Make sure your pet has a complete medical exam by a veterinarian at least once a year.
- Prepare for disasters. Make sure you have a plan for your pet in the event of a hurricane, tornado, fire or flood.
- Plan for your pet's future in case something happens to you and visit *humanesociety.org/petsinwills* for more information.
- Learn how to avoid dog bites, and how to prevent your dog from biting, by going to *humanesociety.org/avoidbites*.

For more information, visit *humanesociety.org*.

Celebrating Animals | Confronting Cruelty

THE HUMANE SOCIETY
OF THE UNITED STATES

1255 23rd Street, NW, Suite 450 • Washington, DC 20037
humanesociety.org

"It's fun to have fun but you have to know how."
—The Cat in the Hat, by Dr. Seuss

TABLE OF CONTENTS

INTRODUCTION

Play is powerful stuff. It influences so many things, including development, motivation, emotions, physiology, communication, and behavior. Wow! That's an impressive list. That's why we believe that play between people and dogs deserves a booklet of its own.

The thoughtful use of play can do much to improve the lives of both people and dogs. Most importantly, play is an effective (and delightful!) way to strengthen our relationships with dogs. Given that people and dogs are members of two different species, what could be more important? We are all used to the idea of being best friends with our dogs, but that relationship shouldn't be taken for granted. Sometimes we forget how special it is. People are amazed to read about individuals of other species who live and play together—a gorilla with a pet kitten, or a dog who raises squirrels, for example—but the fact that we live with dogs isn't considered newsworthy. However, there's no denying that our relationship with dogs is a bit of a miracle, given how closely connected our lives have become.

Our unique relationship with dogs is, in part, a result of our mutual love of play. It is unusual for most animals to play with any regularity when they are adults. There are, of course, exceptions, such as river otters and wolves, but they come to mind partly because we so rarely see mature animals playing. How many grown-up cows have you seen frolicking together around a pasture? People and dogs are exceptions, perhaps because we are what biologists call *neotenous*, meaning that we retain many of our juvenile traits into adulthood.[1] One of those juvenile traits is playfulness, and dogs and people have it in spades—you and your dog are basically modern day Peter Pans. Thus, play is part of our biological bond, and for many of us, part of our day-to-day link with dogs.

---

1 There is some controversy in the scientific community about whether or not dogs are truly neotenous, or whether their juvenile attributes reflect some other phenomena, but that debate is far beyond the scope of this book!

At its simplest, play is fun, and there's nothing like having fun with someone to make you want to spend more time together.

Perhaps this is a good time to ask "what is play, anyway?" Webster's dictionary defines play as "*to occupy oneself in amusement, sport or other recreation: (i.e.) children playing with toys.*" That is a broad definition, encompassing a variety of activities, from playing poker to pole-vaulting to making goofy faces in the mirror. We encourage you to define play broadly too. There are many ways to amuse yourself and your dog; what matters is that the two of you are engaged in an activity that you both enjoy, and that gives you a sense of freedom and lightheartedness. Fetch and chase games are wonderful ways to keep your dog's body well-exercised, and learning new tricks exercises his mind. A balance of mental and physical exercise makes for happy, well-behaved dogs; that's why this booklet includes ways to encourage your dog to use his brain. Games are also great educational tools, and can be used to teach manners to the most exuberant of dogs. Sometimes the best learning happens when it doesn't feel like a "lesson."

You'd think our mutual love of play would mean that we all know how to play together naturally, but people and dogs often miscommunicate while trying to play. What we think of as play signals might be perceived as corrections by some dogs. Or you might be trying to teach your dog one game while he's trying to teach you another—look at how good dogs are at getting us to chase them rather than bringing back the ball! Sometimes, dogs learn things during play sessions that cause problems in other contexts, like nipping the neighbor's child or body-slamming Aunt Nellie. As applied animal behaviorists, we've often seen that happen to nice people with nice dogs who ended up in trouble in spite of themselves. That's not surprising; anything with the power to do good usually comes with the power to do harm. There's no reason that play should be an exception.

Part of what makes play fun is that it can be exciting, but excitement can lead to a lack of emotional control, which, in turn can lead to aggression.

And that's the last thing you want in the middle of a play session with a best friend. Because we want play to be a positive factor in your relationship with your dog, this booklet contains sections that teach you how to play constructive games with your dog as well as sections that help you stay out of trouble.

Every Dog is Different

Just like beauty, the joy of play is in the eyes of the beholder. Although we'll be talking about many kinds of play in this booklet, only some of them will be relevant to you and your dog – every dog is different and every dog enjoys being with his owner in different ways. You can make predictions about a dog's favorite type of play based on his breed, but you might have a retriever who won't retrieve or a terrier who has no interest in playing tug. Some dogs don't seem to want to play at all, preferring the role of noble couch potato to that of class clown. That's okay too; cerebral types often enjoy mental exercise but prefer to leave sports to others.

Before you read any further, consider for a moment the kind of play you do with your dog, how much you each enjoy it, and if there are other kinds of play you can add to your repertoire. Your Aussie may love to play fetch, but might appreciate some mental games thrown in for variety. (Just because you play tennis or golf doesn't mean you don't enjoy crosswords or Sudoku.) Much like kids, some dogs might not know what they like until they try it. We hope to inspire you to try a few new things with your dog. Who knows? Some of them may turn out to be everyone's favorite.

We also encourage you to think about who your dog likes to play with, and when and where he prefers to play. You might have an older dog who takes a while to gear up in the morning—she might be a candidate for games that require exercise later in the day. Perhaps you've noticed that your dog always gravitates toward your teenage son when she's looking for fun. If that's the case, what is your son doing that makes his play so engaging to her? This is a great time to sit back and take stock—spend a few minutes thinking about your dog's play life right now. If you really want to explore the subject, try writing down how, when, and where you play with your dog. There's nothing like writing something down to make things clear, and it's always helpful to know where you're starting.

No matter how or how much your dog likes to play, this booklet is designed to inspire you to incorporate more play into your everyday life. As applied animal behaviorists, we marvel at how much good can result from it. Play can enhance your relationship with your dog, improve your dog's obedience skills, and even prevent and treat behavioral problems. Our goal is to help you use play to make your own life more fun, to have a better-behaved and happier dog, and make the two of you feel even closer than ever in the process.

Play Together, Stay Together is not a comprehensive tome on every possible way to play with your dog. Rather, it is written to inspire you to incorporate different kinds of play into your daily life, to enjoy the benefits of play as a reinforcement for good behavior, and to avoid the kinds of play that can inadvertently lead to trouble. We've tried to keep the booklet short and sweet for one reason—so you can put the book down and start playing!

USING PLAY TO ENHANCE
YOUR RELATIONSHIP

Playing with your dog enriches your relationship with her. It's as simple and as beautiful as that. Many scientific studies on social interactions emphasize the importance of play in good relationships, and that's true of individuals in many species. Across the board, the parents who are the most playful in their interactions with their children have the best relationships with them.[2]

This isn't a surprise to most of us who consider our dogs part of our family, but it's gratifying nonetheless. (And gives you yet another reason to put off cleaning your house and play with your dog instead—see, isn't science fun?) It is also important support for taking play seriously, especially as a way of creating that magically close relationship most of us want to have with our dogs—the animals who share our lives, our homes, and our hearts.

What is surprising is that the type of play we engage in with our dogs is relatively rare in the world of animal behavior. As mentioned earlier, the fact that dogs and humans stay playful as adults is uncommon, and is a significant part of the special relationship we share. To some degree, play isn't what makes our relationship with each other better, play is what creates the relationship in the first place. That's powerful stuff.

Decoding the way play influences relationships and how relationships influence play has kept social scientists busy for decades. Heaven knows there's still a lot to learn. What we do know is that people play most with those they feel close to and with whom they feel comfortable. There is no

2 See the Resource section for references.

reason to think this basic truth breaks down when considered across species lines, and recent research suggests it is true for dogs as well as people. A study by Topál and others found that dogs are more likely to play with a stranger when their owners are present then when the owners are not. Dogs usually don't initiate play when they are around people who make them nervous. (Come to think of it, we're not playful when we're nervous around an unfamiliar dog.) However, play can be a wonderful way to increase everyone's comfort level, whether it's a shy dog playing fetch with an unfamiliar visitor or a cautious little boy throwing the ball for a big dog.

According to a study by Rooney and Bradshaw, play sessions can help make training more effective. They found that dogs scored higher in "obedient attentiveness" after a play session than they did prior to it. This is no surprise to many trainers and owners, as it simply confirms what most of us already know: Training is often easier and more effective immediately after we have played with our dogs. Whether it is the exercise, the fun, or some other aspect of play is hard to know, but play gets our dogs' attention. The extra attentiveness lasts beyond the play session itself, and no matter what the reason, that is most definitely good for our relationship.

Although there is little research on the effects of different types of play on canine behavior, one of Rooney and Bradshaw's studies suggests that games with a lot of physical contact may affect attachment, as well as implying a correlation between these sorts of games and separation-related behavior. They had owners play with their dogs and then leave the room, and compared the types of play with the dog's behavior once the owner had departed. The authors found that lots of physical contact during the play session correlated with less anxiety-related behavior once the owner had gone. (Examples of such behaviors include the dog staying by the door through which his owner had just left, or vocalizing in the owner's absence.) Since the study only addressed correlations, it is impossible to know whether certain games directly influence our dogs' attachment to us, but it is worth considering that increased physical contact during play may have an impact.

We do have a caveat, however. Even though there seems to be a benefit to physical play with your dog, we caution you against wrestle play (see "How Not to Play With Your Dog," p. 73), which can lead to a raft of problems. Your best bet is to play in other, more gentle ways.

Telling Your Dog You Want to Play

Our mutual love of play doesn't always mean that we know how to play well together. After all, we are two different species, and it's not surprising that we occasionally miscommunicate. Sometimes that simply means that the dog doesn't bring back the ball, but other times, it can result in dangerous or frightening situations. Misunderstandings during play are a realistic concern, because social play consists primarily of actions borrowed from fighting, predation, and courtship. Predatory behavior patterns—such as chasing, biting, and shaking—are especially problematic; all of these actions are highly arousing and potentially dangerous if things get out of hand.

That is why dogs have evolved stereotypical play signals that can be roughly translated as "I'm just fooling, honest!" Dogs do things during play sessions that would be considered antagonistic in other contexts, so it's critical that their behavior is perceived by their canine playmates as friendly rather than aggressive. People are no different—imagine if what you see on a football field happened in a supermarket parking lot between strangers. Thus, the purpose of play signals is to make sure that all participants understand that what is going on is playful, not threatening.

Because dogs need and expect their play partners to communicate clearly, it is worthwhile thinking about the signals they use and how we can incorporate them into our own repertoires. The classic play signal is the play bow, and it's a common sight wherever happy, well-adjusted dogs congregate. One dog plunks down the front part of his body so he is perched on his elbows, while his back end remains at near-normal elevation. Perhaps another dog assumes this same position before they race off together in a merry game of chase. What fun! What joy! The game is afoot!

Play bows are used to initiate play and also during play to keep it going. Many dogs wag their tails, and some bark while performing a play bow, but the basic form is always the same: The front part of the body is low, and the back end is higher. Lowering the head may allow a dog who wants to play appear to be less threatening than would otherwise be the case. The fact that play bows are so consistent in their form probably relates to how important it is for play signals to be unambiguous.

Although there is no definitive research on this, it is also likely that play bows function to create pauses in the vigorous nature of social play. In appropriate play, dogs often stop for a brief moment and then resume, alternating chasing, batting, and mouthing with play bows and standing still. These pauses create breaks in the high-energy, high-arousal kind of play that can lead to over arousal and eventually to trouble. These pauses are so important that we can use them to determine whether or not dogs are playing appropriately. Dogs who have the self-control to take a break are most likely the ones able to avoid over arousal, loss of impulse control, and inappropriate responses to the behavior of their partners.

The importance of pauses and breaks in dog play are the reason that it is critical to play with your dog in an "off and on" kind of way. Ignoring the need to take pauses, and thus to allow emotions to settle, is a common problem in play between people and dogs (especially between children and dogs). We're not saying you need to do your own play bows, but it is crucial to alternate vigorous play with short breaks to keep emotions in check. A perfect example of doing that is described in the tug-game section in which you teach your dog to play hard and then pause as a way of teaching emotional control.

Although there's much to be learned, there has been little research on how dogs perceive our attempts to signal that we want to play. A study by Rooney, Bradshaw, and Robinson investigated dogs' responses to human play signals. They found that although people can indeed communicate a desire to play to their dogs, the most common ways that people try to do that are not necessarily the most successful. For example, patting the floor and whispering were both frequently used by people attempting to initiate play with their dogs, but dogs often didn't respond playfully to either of those signals.[3] In contrast, two other human signals—running toward or away from the dog, as well as tapping their own chests—were highly effective at initiating play with dogs. However, people didn't tend to use these very often.

In their study, the *least* effective human behaviors for eliciting play in dogs were kissing the dog, picking up the dog, and barking at the dog, none of which ever resulted in play. Stamping one's feet and pulling the dog's tail (sigh) had very low rates of playful response by the dogs. The human signals that most frequently elicited play were the forward lunge (the person makes a sudden quick movement toward the dog, which is much like what are called "start-stops" in dog-dog play), the vertical bow (the person bends at the waist until the torso is horizontal, or a human version of the play bow), a "real" or full play bow, chasing the dog or running away from the dog, and grabbing the dog's paws (which we don't recommend!). The study also found that play signals were more successful at eliciting play when accompanied by vocalizations.

Of course, one of the most common and effective ways to start playing with your dog is to pick up a toy (which was not included in the study cited). Whether you then toss it, hold it out toward your dog for him to grab, or call out "Wanna play?", most dogs know that when you pick up a toy, play time has begun.

Play faces are another signal that easily translates across species. Play faces usually involve a circular, open mouth; open eyes; relaxed facial muscles and ears; and raised eyebrows. To make yourself appear more playful to your dog, you, too, can mimic a canine play face by displaying an open-mouthed grin, open eyes, and relaxed facial muscles. We're not quite sure what to say about relaxing your ears—if you figure out how to do it, let us know.

---

3 FYI, patting the floor is a great way to help your dog lie down on cue—no wonder it doesn't work as a play signal!

Play signals between our two species can sometimes be effective, but in other cases, they're just confusing. For example, many dogs jump up on people, who respond by pushing the dog away with their hands. In the canine world, pushing with paws, or "boxing," is a playful behavior that often incites further play. In this case, the dog thinks the person is being playful, and responds with more leaps and jumps. The person responds with more pushing away, perhaps even more energetically out of irritation, which the dog takes as a signal for more vigorous play. This cycle can go on until the person angrily yells at the dog or gets up and walks away. The poor dog probably thought they were having such a nice time playing together, and is now totally perplexed. You can see why a thorough knowledge of canine play signals can help you avoid confusion and ensure that your play sessions are fun for all.

And now ... let the games begin!

GAMES TO PLAY WITH YOUR DOG

The following section emphasizes fun and constructive ways to play with your dog, based on the natural behavior of both species. Think of this section as a basic guide to happy and healthy play between the two of you.

The Chase Game

Dogs come to us with a built-in love of the chase. That's why they are called cursorial predators—they evolved from animals whose lives depended on their ability to run after prey. Most dogs still consider a good chase to be the world's coolest game, as you can see when you watch two dogs playing. A big part of play between dogs includes lots of running, with one dog saying "Catch me if you can!" and the other running hard to do just that. Look at the faces of dogs when they're playing—it's hard to find a happier expression than that of a dog engrossed in a chase game. But why leave all the fun to the dogs? Teaching your dog that you can play the chase game is a powerful way to enhance your relationship. We suspect that if dogs could talk about their owners, they'd whine about how incredibly, boringly slow we are. "Why don't they ever run? They are SO SLOW!" (Remember saying this about your parents when you were a child?) We envision dogs everywhere lighting up with joy when their owners finally start playing "right" by engaging in chase games like proper playmates. Finally, humans have figured out how to have a good time!

You can play the chase game anywhere, and you don't have to have a toy or a treat in your pocket (although that never hurts) or be a runner to enjoy it.[4] If you have a hallway or a big room suitable for drag racing, you can even do this inside. All you need to do is clap or "smooch" to get your dog's attention, then take off running away from him as soon as he looks at you. We like to clap as we run; giggles are optional, but they make it more fun. Of course, the best place to play chase with your dog is outside in an area where you know your dog is safe off-leash. That gives you room to run ten yards one way and then sprint off in another direction before your dog catches up.

Even though the basics are pretty simple, there are a few things to keep in mind to keep this game safe and effective. Read this next section carefully before you add "cursorial" to your own resume.

One Way Only. Most importantly, your chase games should only go in one direction—always run away from your dog. Unlike dogs playing at a dog park, you shouldn't alternate roles between the chaser and the chasee. We know that some people delight in chasing after their dogs, and we hate to be a wet blanket, but here's the deal—if you run after your dog, you are going to condition him to run away from you when you move toward him. Dogs respond to tiny movements, and if you chase your dog, he'll learn that your first step toward him is going to be followed by lots more. Eventually, he'll cut to the chase (so to speak) as soon as you lean toward him, and he'll take off running away from you. That will happen when you merely lean toward him to put on his leash at the dog park, so be forewarned.

The good news is that you can use your dog's keen observational skills to your advantage. After you've let him chase you for a few weeks, you can simply turn your body as if to run away and your dog will run to you. Say "Georgie, come!" right before you turn, and you can substantially improve your dog's responsiveness when you call him.

---

4 We say thank heavens for that! Karen runs miles on a daily basis, but although Patricia loves to hike, her body thinks running more than twenty yards is abusive.

Know When to Stop. You also want to be sure that the chase game doesn't turn into the "nip-my-owner-on-the-leg" game. Dogs may come hard-wired to chase things, but some also come with a tendency to grab them with their mouths when they catch them. Some dogs are a lot more mouthy than others, but you always want to stop before your dog catches up to you. When he is four or five feet away, turn toward him and reinforce him with a treat, a toy, or the beginning of another chase game. Exactly when you stop running depends on your dog; some dogs will need you to stop sooner than others. Your goal is to encourage your dog to run toward you without causing him to get mouthy. This is especially important for children, who aren't capable of controlling their own excitement and can be hurt in chase games with dogs. That's why we strongly recommend that only adults and children over the age of twelve or fourteen be allowed to play this game.

We should mention that not all dogs have read the chapters on canine ethology, and some are not aware that they are supposed to love running. Some dogs just don't like to run, simple as that. You can make generalities—herding dogs like to run more than lap dogs, young dogs like to run more than older dogs—but each dog is an individual. If you're not sure how much your dog loves to run, just go outside in a safe fenced area and let your dog off leash. After he's had a few minutes to sniff around, clap your hands and run away while he's looking at you. If you try that several times when there is little else to distract him and he responds by standing and staring at you, the chase game probably isn't going to be much fun for either of you. Still, with the occasional exception, most dogs do love to run, and that's something all of us can do without any training. You know how to run already, you have all the equipment you need to do it—just remember to run away from your dog and stop before he catches up to you.

It works especially well to intersperse chase games with obedience exercises and other types of play. (See, for example, page 54 on using chase to teach coming when called.) You don't need to run far, perhaps ten yards one way, then five in another direction, and then eight yards back toward where you came from. It's amazing how little of this you need to do to stimulate your dog. Running is so much fun for them that once you start, you have their undivided attention. You can make the chase game even more interesting by giving your dog a treat once he catches up (don't have him sit every time—if you do, the treat is for sitting, not running to you) or by tossing a toy behind you. If you do toss a toy, don't throw it in the direction your dog came from; that will teach him to stop short in anticipation. Throw it through your legs (okay, not if you have a Great Dane) or behind you, or wave it in front of his face and take off running again.

Play Ball!

Toys are a big part of our relationship with dogs—our shared fascination with all things bouncy, squeaky, and floppy makes us natural playmates. Playing with toys, whether with two- or four-legged friends, is so common that it seems unremarkable to us, but "object play" is rare in the world of adult mammals. You wouldn't know it by watching people and dogs play together, though, as we mutually fixate on balls, flying discs, and retrievable plush squeaky toys. And the best interactive game with toys—the game of fetch—provides your dog with lots of exercise and makes you literally the best game in town.

However, in spite of the popularity of retrieving games, we humans often have trouble getting it to work as we'd like. It seems dogs would rather that we did the actual fetching, and they are masters at teaching us to do so! That's why the following section describes in detail how to ensure that your dog is the one doing the running and retrieving. If she isn't interested in toys at all, and that's fine by you, no problem. Simply skip to the next section. However, if you'd like to play fetch with this kind of dog, here's how to get her started. Try stuffing a hollow toy with food for a few weeks and tossing it three or four feet away from her. Let her go after it, but let her settle down with it if that's what she wants. Your goal is to get her started running toward a toy you've tossed; don't worry yet about the retrieving part. Do this several times a day for several weeks, and then start tossing the same toy without food and encouraging her to go after it. Once you've gotten to that point, you can follow along with the instructions below.

For the rest of us, whose dogs are crazed to chase after things, here's the way to play with them without bringing out a bottomless bucket of balls.

Teaching Your Dog to Fetch (Instead of Vice Versa!). It seems as though what dogs really want to play is "Tag, you're it!" and have you chase them around the yard. They want to get the toy in their mouth and have you run after them while they chant some doggy equivalent of "Na ne na ne boo boo! I've got the ba-a-all!" If you want to learn how to be a great animal trainer, watch a dog teach a person a fetch game in reverse. Dogs are masters at training us, and we all can learn from their example. Here are some ideas to try to turn the tables on them.

Let's say you're teaching your dog Lady to bring back the ball. Start by waving a ball about two feet in front of her face (not too close or you'll push her away). It's often the movement that attracts dogs more than the object, so get her focused on the ball by moving it back and forth, or bouncing it a couple of times and then tossing it no more than four or five feet away. If she trots to it and puts her mouth around it, softly clap your hands and run the other way, encouraging her to move toward you. Wait to clap until she has it in her mouth, and resist the urge to say her name or call her to come—this causes many dogs to drop the ball and trot obediently to you. (Do not be distracted by the hysterical laughter of other readers whose dogs pick up the ball and run a hundred yards away in response to hearing their name or the word "Come.")

If she comes partway to you with the ball in her mouth and then stops and tries to get you to chase her, back up again, clap some more and run *away* from her to lure her toward you. This game has one rule that can't be broken: She moves toward you, you never move toward her. If your dog is one of those who grabs the ball and runs, start running yourself, but always *in the opposite direction*. It's a rare dog who can resist a chase game, and it's up to you to decide who is the chaser and who is the chasee. This isn't always easy—you have to make a conscious effort not to give in and run after your dog—but it'll pay off in the long run.

If she does bring the ball toward you and drops it anywhere near your feet, pick it up and throw it *instantly*. Most of us tend to pick up the ball, hold it in our hot little paws, and either ask our dogs to sit, spend several seconds praising them, or pet their heads when they'd rather we didn't. We call this playing fetch. Dogs call it hoarding. They want the ball back, period. So give it to them! Throw the ball *the instant* your dog drops it. This sounds simple, but after years of experience, we can tell you that people need lots of coaching on this. When you begin teaching your dog to fetch, either focus on throwing the ball as though it were a hot potato or have someone watch you and shout "throw it!" the second you get your hands on it.

Most young dogs will only fetch a few times, so don't be discouraged if Lady brings the ball back twice and then stops. This is especially common outside where there are so many distractions. If Lady brings the ball back two times and then puts it down and ignores it, that's okay. Game over. Quietly go get the ball and end the play session. If you notice a pattern (say, she fetches five times in a row and then quits), stop the game the next time after four throws and leave her wanting more.

The most common fetching problem is a dog who brings the ball back but won't give it up. She wants you to want it, oh yes she does, but there is no way she is going to give it up. Here's where you need to beat her at the "hard-to-get" game. As soon as she's anywhere near you, fold your arms and turn away from her, refusing to face her or to reach for the ball. Dogs who love the game will keep trying to face you, and many of them will eventually drop the ball. If that happens, swoop it up and throw it as soon as you can.

If your dog won't drop the ball no matter how long you play hard-to-get, try tossing a second ball once she has approached with the first. Most dogs will drop the ball in their mouths as soon as a second one is thrown. It can take a while to convince a dog to drop the first ball without a second one, but if you continue this throughout several weeks or months, you'll end up with a dog who reliably fetches without the addition of a "back-up ball." You can also swap the ball for a treat you've kept in your pocket, saying "Drop it" just before you wave the food under your dog's nose. Give her the treat, then pick up the ball that's been dropped to get the food, and toss it again. (See "Take It/Drop It" on page 61 for more on teaching dogs to drop on cue.[5]) Some dogs lose interest in the ball if they learn you have treats, but trading a treat for the ball works well for the ones who are committed retrievers. It won't take long before you can eliminate the treat altogether, because chasing the ball is more than enough reinforcement for giving it back to you.

The keys to teaching fetch are to move away from your dog to encourage her to come to you, to reinforce anything she does that approximates fetching at first, and to ignore her attempts to teach you to play "Chase the dog around the yard."

The next section contains another great way to use toys to play with your dog: playing tug, which is without a doubt many canines' favorite game of all time.

---

5 We prefer the term "cue," which is more commonly used by professional trainers, instead of the antiquated word "command." It may seem trivial, but language reflects attitude and we are not so much ordering our dogs around by "commanding them" as we are informing them about what to do.

The Tug Game

Tug can be a wonderful addition to your repertoire. Most dogs love to play tug, and no one has to teach them how to do it. Even young puppies play tug games when they are barely old enough to walk. You don't meet many dogs who "sort of like" to play tug—they either have no interest in it or they LOVE it, and that makes it a powerful reinforcement for the ones who do.

The Benefits of Playing Tug. Playing tug has many benefits to both you and your dog. It's a great way to exercise your dog (and you too, since even a small dog can give you quite a workout), and a good way to help dogs work off steam. Walks around the neighborhood are great, but strolling down the sidewalk at a normal walking pace is barely enough to elevate the heartbeat of a healthy dog. Tug games can provide lots of high-intensity exercise, even in your living room. If it's five below zero, or ninety-five degrees and humid outside, being able to stay inside while you play is surely a good thing.

Another benefit of tug is that neither one of you needs any training to get it started. Who needs to practice "Pick up object, let dog take in mouth. Pull. Pull harder."? It can take some practice to ensure that excitable dogs don't become overly aroused, but surely tug is one of the most natural and rewarding games shared by people and dogs. Some dogs, however, don't take to it as naturally as you might think. Submissive dogs, especially, can be cautious about pulling back on an object as soon as you pick it up. The trick is to signal to your dog that you want to play—try a modified play bow—then shake a long toy on the ground to attract his attention. Let the end of the toy closest to your dog twitch around like a dancing mouse, and praise quietly every time he moves toward it. Once he takes it in his mouth, pull back very gently at first, continuing to praise if he pulls back against you. If your dog is super sound-sensitive, stay silent or add some quiet, encouraging "Good boys!" to help him stay engaged.

Concerns About Playing Tug. Tug games haven't always been popular with trainers—for years we were advised not to play tug with our dogs. (Even Patricia cautioned against it twenty years ago. Sigh.) As is often the case, knowledge and beliefs change over time, and tug is now one of the most popular ways professional trainers reinforce their dogs with play.

Historical concerns about playing tug included worries about teaching dogs to use the full force of their mouth around people, the effect of "winning" if the dog got the toy, and worries about dogs becoming overly aroused. More recently, some have argued that tug games were fine as long as the dog didn't win the game and end up with the toy. In this case, the concern was that the dog would perceive himself as higher in social status than the people in the house, and thus be empowered to start to throwing his weight around.

However, some interesting research by Rooney and Bradshaw supports the addition of tug games to our repertoires. Their work suggests that keeping possession of a toy after a game of tug has no impact on the relative status of a human-dog pair. But it also suggests that we might want to be thoughtful about letting certain dogs keep the toy after a game of tug. Rooney and Bradshaw found that the most playful dogs in the study were pushier about getting attention from their owners when they were allowed to "win" by keeping the toy. Thus, it might be better not to allow persistent dogs—the kind who pester you to play JUST ONE MORE TIME—to prance off with that slimy rope toy after the two of you are done playing.

Be Careful Your Dog Doesn't Become Overly Excited. The one historical concern about tug games that still deserves attention is the worry about dogs becoming overly aroused while playing. If not handled properly, this can indeed become a problem. Tug involves a dog using the full force of his mouth, the one with the big teeth in it, to rip and tear at something to which you are attached. Dogs can get so excited that they forget the difference between a tug toy and your hand, which pretty much means the fun is over for one of you. The flip side of this potential problem is that you can use tug to teach your dog emotional control, and it's a wonderful way to teach a dog to drop something—anything—in response to a quiet cue from you. Both of those are important social skills in family dogs, just as they are in people. Tug games allow you to control the situation and reinforce your dog for keeping his emotions in check, or for giving up an object he really, really wants to have. Thus, you can use tug to exercise your dog and to teach him many valuable lessons. It's great way to have fun and multitask at the same time. (See "Tug and Teaching Take It/ Drop It" on page 61 and "Teach Your Dog to Chill" on page 63 for specific information about how to incorporate these lessons into your tug games. "Know the Signs of Over Arousal" (page 79) has tips to help you monitor your dog's emotional thermostat.)

Avoid Injuries. It's always best to pull straight back rather than whipping your dog's head back and forth as she holds on. It's fine for her to shake her head herself, but go easy when you are doing the pulling—you can cause or exacerbate neck injuries if you're not careful.

Tug Toys. It's a good idea to have some designated tug toys, and to keep them out of your dog's reach except at play time. That increases their value, and decreases the chance that your dog will start a tug game with any object he picks up (like your favorite sweater when it falls on the floor). The best tug toys are long ones—long enough to keep your hands well away from the dog's mouth. The gentlest of dogs can inadvertently hurt you by trying to get a better grip on the toy and ending up gripping something else instead. Like your fingers. Ouch.

Needless to say, this section is only relevant for dogs who love to play with objects and would enjoy playing tug games with you. If your dog isn't fond of toys, then skip to the next games. But if your dog loves toys, tug can be your dog's favorite game of all.

The Crazy Owner Game

You wouldn't normally think of walking your dog on leash as play, but changing the way you approach it can create a fun, interactive game for you and your dog. Why let that daily activity be the "same-ole, same-ole," when you could turn it into a silly diversion? Walking your dog provides a great opportunity to add play to your daily routine, and to convince your dog that you really are the best owner in the world.

Here's what you need to do: Take a handful of small, yummy treats with you on your walk. Lure your dog to your left side by letting him sniff the hand that has some goodies in it, and then start to walk away. Offer praise and give him a treat every time he's walking beside you, or looking at you instead of sniffing the grass. You're not necessarily trying to teach heel here (although this game can significantly improve your dog's leash manners), you're just trying to get his attention and teach him that you are as interesting as the smells in the grass.

Once your dog has discovered that there's a silly game afoot, start playing the "crazy owner game." No funny hats are required—simply vary your speed and direction often, so your dog can't predict what you're going to do next. Instead of walking in a straight line at the same pace, you want to go fast, then slow, then right, then left. This unpredictable behavior means your dog never quite knows what to expect, and it makes you very interesting indeed! Continue to give your dog treats every few steps at first, but use them more sparingly as you progress. As long as your behavior is interesting, and the treats and praise come on occasion, your dog is going to think of this as yet another wonderful game you play together.

Here's what one session might look like: Imagine you've walked forward three quick steps. Your rapid movement got your dog's attention, so he moved along with you. Give him some hearty praise and a tasty treat. Now stride forward for five steps, but take long loping steps. Stop for a second, tell your dog how cute he is, and then turn right and take two quick, little steps. Give him a treat, and then go forward rapidly for five or six strides; then, without stopping, turn right and slow down again, then turn 180 degrees around your left side, or in front of your dog, and take two more steps. (You see now why we used to have T-shirts illustrating this game and saying, "I'm not crazy. I'm just training my dog!"). It's guaranteed to bring your neighbors to their windows.

Of course, the example above is just an illustration. Exactly how you do this doesn't matter, as long as your dog starts to learn that you are unpredictable (read "interesting") and you don't wrap yourself and your dog up in the leash like cartoon characters. You'll need to modify what you do based on your dog's responses, much as though you and your dog were partners in a dance. In some senses, you are—you lead, he follows. Some dogs will get too excited if you go forward too fast, and so you'll need to moderate your "fast" strides. Other dogs who like to forge ahead will trip you up if you try to turn in front of them to the left. If that's happening to you, just turn the other way so that your dog is behind you, then turn left in front of him again before he catches up.

On every walk, intersperse this game with plenty of time for your dog to sniff and explore the area— after all, every dog deserves time to be a dog and use his nose! You'd be wise to put this game on cue so your dog knows exactly when it's game time and when it's appropriate for him to take his attention off you. You might say "Crazy Game!" when you begin your random pattern of walking, and "Okay" or "Free" when it's time for him to have a bit more freedom. Again, your goal here is not to teach your dog to do a formal heel, although most people find this game results in a dog with remarkably better leash manners. It's the perfect multi-tasking— you get the dog walked and the dog learns that paying attention to you is an entertaining pastime.

The Find It Game

A great game for keeping your dog occupied is the Find It game. You can teach your dog to find some treats, to find his ball, or to find any other object you want him to search for. Some dogs learn best if you teach them this game with treats, although toy-crazy canines may prefer to play the game with toys.

We'll start with the food hounds first: Put some treats on the floor or furniture near you without your dog seeing you do it. You can put two or three down at the same time, perhaps about three feet apart. Say "Find your treats!" in a cheerful voice and tap your toe or use your finger to point to the treats. Despite their amazing sense of smell, most dogs will first use their eyes to find the treats; eventually, they learn to sniff around to find them. Once your dog starts to look (or sniff) for the treats after you say the cue, drop the tapping or pointing motion. As your dog gets better at finding the treats, start increasing the distance between them, always placing the treats when your dog isn't watching. You can increase the difficulty by putting the treats all over an entire room or throughout several rooms in your house, or by making the hiding spots trickier. You can even do it out in your yard.

If you play this game as "Find your Kong®" or "Find your ball," the best reinforcement for your dog's success is to play with him. You can play with him the instant he finds the toy, or you can head outside for a play session. What could be more natural after you tell him to go find a toy? If you play this game with toys, you have the added option of teaching your dog the names of all of his toys so you can tell him "Find your disc," or "Find your bunny." Some dogs can learn the names of many different objects, which can make this game an entertaining challenge for them.

In addition to giving your dog something fun to do that uses his mind and his sensory abilities, there are other benefits to this game as well. If you drop a piece of food or a treat and can't find it, ask your dog to do it for you. He can help you find his toys if they get lost, which no doubt happens to everybody's favorite toy from time to time. If you put your dog on a stay while you hide the treats or toys, you can even work in some obedience while you play.

As wonderful as this game is, it's not for every dog. We don't advise playing it with dogs who guard food or toys because the dog may miss something on the first pass and find it when you inadvertently reach toward it. Speaking of food being left lying in as-yet-undiscovered hiding places, be sure to use dry treats for this game rather than spoilable wet stuff, for reasons that are no doubt obvious. One last caution: Some dogs learn to search for food in your house even when you are not playing the game, and that may not be desirable for everyone. For years, Karen could leave her treat-filled workbag lying around anywhere and her dog never got into it. A couple of weeks after teaching him to play this game, his days of ignoring the bag were over. If the bag was left out, he found the treats inside. Be forewarned!

Hide and Seek

If you want to make your local dog trainer ecstatic beyond all expectation, simply mention that you play hide and seek with your dog. Despite the fact that all trainers have different perspectives about how to train dogs, you'd be hard pressed to find one using positive methods who has anything but praise for this game. It incorporates recall practice in a way that is fun and reinforcing for your dog, has an element of the joy of discovery, and teaches your dog to come when called even if he can't see you. This game also teaches your dog to pay enough attention to you that he knows where you are at all times, even while walking off-leash. Those are a lot of benefits from a pretty simple game!

To teach your dog how to play hide and seek, start by calling him to come when you are partly out of sight. You could stand with half of your body showing behind a door, or duck behind something too small to conceal you, such as a mop bucket or foot stool. Say "Come!" and then clap, smooch, say pup-pup-pup, or rattle his favorite bag of dog treats to get him to run over to you. Once he finds you, reinforce him with top-quality treats, toss a new chew toy, or run away so he can chase you. Be prepared to reinforce him right away—it will be too late if you have to jump up to get treats from the cupboard.

As your dog learns to find you, you can hide more completely—behind a door, in another room, in the bathtub, or behind the couch—and increase the difficulty of the game. Karen once got stuck in a laundry hamper while playing this game, but her dog did find her! Be creative and vary your hiding places.

You can play outside, too, as long as you're in a safe area. To maximize the benefit of teaching your dog to find you, drop out of sight and call him just as he notices he's lost you. Choose a spot behind a tree or shrub, slip at least partially out of sight and then call your dog to come. If your hiding place is too hard, it is possible that your dog will get frustrated, or in rare cases, panicky. Therefore, be sure to increase the difficulty of your hiding places gradually, and make yourself more visible if your dog seems upset by your absence. Some dogs may not care so much about your absence, especially outdoors in a really interesting place, but the clingy ones get wild-eyed if they think they've lost you. But oh the joy of having a dog who learns to pay attention to where you are!

A special case of hide and seek is called "family circle," and it is played by several people at once with the dog. It has the additional benefit of teaching your dog the names of different people, and even to go get them for you when you need them.

It's an easy game to play: One person says, "Where's Ian?" and then Ian claps his hands and encourages the dog to run to him. If the dog goes to the right person, he's reinforced, but if he goes to somebody else, he's ignored. Once Ian has reinforced the dog, he says, "Where's Kelly?" and then Kelly calls the dog to come. Only if the dog goes to Kelly is he reinforced. Be careful though—it is easy to inadvertently teach a dog to run to people in a specific order rather than listening to the names called. You can prevent that by varying the order of the names called, and working with different people at different times. If you always play with the same two people, "Where's —?" can come to mean "go to the other person."

TEACHING TRICKS

Dogs love to do tricks if they are taught with patience and lots of positive reinforcement. And why not? They get lots of treats for doing them, and just as importantly, our attitude is often different when we're teaching them. Because tricks are usually categorized as "silly games we play with our dogs" instead of "obedience," we tend to get less upset if our dogs don't comply. It's easy to feel discouraged when we say "down" and our dog doesn't respond. But what if our dog doesn't do a trick? What do we do? Most of us just shrug our shoulders and laugh. "Oh well," we say. "I guess we won't win the trick contest on *Animal Planet*!" No wonder so many dogs love trick training. Their humans are usually much more fun when they're teaching them.

There are multitudes of great tricks you can teach your dog, and we can't begin to do them justice here. That's why we have our favorite trick books listed in the Resources section. We are including just a few here as inspiration for great things to come. We chose five tricks that any healthy dog can do, that are relatively easy to train, and that we think are charming. Some of these tricks are adapted from *101 Dog Tricks*, an inspiring book that makes us want to retire and spend all of our free time teaching tricks to anything with four legs.

Jump Through a Hoop

There's something endearing about a dog jumping through a hoop—it seems to charm the pants off of everyone, even people who aren't all that fond of dogs. It's also a wonderful trick for children to teach, as long as they are old enough to avoid compromising the safety of your dog. Dogs seem to get into the game too; they are able to generalize jumping through anything round after awhile, and you can create a variety of tricks from the simplest of starts. Patricia used a similar technique to teach her first Border Collie to jump over her back, and people who saw it when they were children still talk about it now that they're in their late twenties. All that's necessary is to ensure that your dog is healthy and that jumping won't cause or aggravate an injury. If you have any concerns about that, you'd be wise to talk to your vet before proceeding.

Start by purchasing a hula hoop, but be sure it doesn't have noisy beads in it—they might frighten your dog. (You can remove the beads by cutting a small hole in the hoop with a carpet knife and shaking them out.) Place the hoop in a doorway, with the bottom touching the ground, and toss a treat through it to encourage your dog to run through. Once he's happy to run through it, say "Hup!" before he gets to the hoop. (Putting the hoop in the doorway will prevent your dog from going around it to get the treat. To get it, he *has* to go through the hoop.) Next, raise the hoop so that it is just an inch or two off the ground, toss the treat through it, and say "Hup" just before your dog moves through the hoop. Be sure to toss the treat far enough past the hoop so that he doesn't stop to get it as soon as he lands—it should travel a good five feet beyond the hoop. Gradually raise the height of the hoop, but resist the urge to go too high, too fast. You'll do better by going slowly and building a solid foundation of success rather than teaching him to run under the hoop because you raised it too quickly. Keep the hoop no more than six or nine inches above the ground for the first six or eight sessions.

After your dog is jumping through the hoop when it's six inches off the ground, move it a foot away from the door, but place it lower to the floor to make it easy for your dog to win. Gradually hold it higher or farther away from the door, but work on one challenge at a time—if the hoop is farther away from the door, lower it a bit. If you want to try for a higher jump, go closer to the door. Asking for easier jumps when you move the hoop away from the door will make it less likely that he will go around the hoop instead of through it. Caution: Don't ask your dog to jump higher than he is able, and remember that he'll need a running start to do a higher jump. You can ask him to sit and stay five to ten feet away from the jump, and then say "Hup!"

Once you have your dog jumping confidently through a hoop, you can invent all kinds of other games. Teach your dog to jump through your arms, or have him jump through the hoop above your leg, and then turn it into a jump over your leg, or even your back. You can do silly things with the hoop like put crepe paper on it to make it a "flaming hoop." This game can be played with any size dog just about anywhere, so we highly recommend adding it to your repertoire.

Aren't You Ashamed of Yourself?

This is a great parlor trick, and one that will make you and your friends laugh on the darkest of days. Your dog will hide his head under a pillow or blanket when you say "Aren't you ashamed of yourself?" It takes more training than jumping through a hoop, but it's not that hard for most dogs, and it's such a great trick to show off to your friends that it's worth the effort. Start by putting a treat under a cushion or folded blanket that your dog can push his nose under. A cushion tied to the back of a wooden chair can work well if it's at your dog's nose level, but Patricia had the most luck with a doggie sleeping pad placed on the ground, so we'll use that as an example. Show your dog a treat, and then put the hand with the treat underneath the pad, a few inches from your dog's nose, and say "Good boy!" as he finds it and eats it. Once he starts shoving his nose under the pad with vigor, say "Aren't you ashamed of yourself?" in a silly, teasing voice as soon as you've placed the treat. (Don't use a "shaming" voice at this point—you don't want your dog to really feel ashamed!)

As you progress, move the treat farther back toward the rear of the pad to encourage him to place his entire head underneath it. Once he's enthusiastically pushing his head under the pad, slide your treat hand in from the other side. That means you and the dog are on opposite sides, with the pad between you. It's important to move to the other side as soon as you can so that he won't be tempted to slip his head out and look back at you if you are behind him. Give him the treat as soon as his head is entirely covered.

Once he'll push his head completely under the pad, move to the next phase. Insert the treat as usual, but don't release it—keep your hand wrapped around it so he can't get it. Pause for a second or two, but no longer, so that he doesn't give up and bring his head out to look for it. Over several sessions, start asking him to hold his head in place for longer periods of time, eventually up to three to five seconds, before releasing the treat.

The last step is to say "Aren't you ashamed of yourself?" and wait for your dog to hide his head himself without you having to slide a treat under the pad to entice him. It will help him immensely if you stand (or sit) in the same place as before, and keep everything else consistent. Just move to your usual side, give him his cue, and position yourself as you have before, holding the treat in your hand. Be ready to reinforce him—always on the other side of the pad and underneath it—as soon as he offers you the behavior. Eventually, you can stand well away from the pad and ask the question. Be sure to give him extra praise and rewards at first if he does the trick when you're standing in a different place than usual.

I Need a Hanky

You sneeze, your dog brings you a handkerchief or a tissue—this is another trick with off-the-chart charm value. Of course, it's a lot easier if your dog already fetches objects, but it's such a fun trick we couldn't leave it out. Your dog will need to know "Take It" first. (If he doesn't, see the Tug and Teaching Take It/Drop It section on page 61.)

Bringing the Hanky. Once your dog will take something on cue and give it to you when asked, you can ask him to pick up a tissue or a handkerchief. Some dogs might be hesitant to bring you an actual tissue—either they've been discouraged from raiding the tissue box or it just doesn't taste good. If that's the case with your dog, try using cloth handkerchiefs, or rolling up a tissue and tossing it like a ball. Many dogs are encouraged to pick up a cloth handkerchief if you roll it around a hard biscuit. Reinforce your dog with treats for catching the object or picking it up from the floor, even if he spits it out right away. Once he's catching it readily, ask him to take it from your hand (try showing it to him and then snatching it away a few times—"hard to get" works on dogs too!) Gradually up the ante so that he holds the cloth or tissue in his mouth for a second, then two, and eventually walks a few steps with it in his mouth. This will take one quick session for some dogs, and several sessions for others.

Making Your Sneeze the Cue. Now that your dog will take a handkerchief from your hand and hold it in his mouth (we'll use the cloth version just to avoid repetition, but you can substitute tissue if you'd rather use that), put it partway into your pocket, or into a tissue box you've attached to a low table with duct tape. Sneeze with a clear ACHOO! and then say "Take it" while you encourage your dog by pointing or moving the top of the cloth to direct his attention. Reinforce anything approximating what you want, even if he just goes over to the handkerchief and mouths it for a moment. Be very clear about what you're reinforcing him for—say "Good!" or click the instant he does what you'd like him to. Once he's readily bringing the handkerchief back, phase out the "Take it" cue and use only ACHOO! as your cue. If necessary, see the instructions in Tug and Teaching Take It/Drop It to encourage your dog to offer you the handkerchief and let you take it out of his mouth. Over time, expect him to do more and more of the entire trick until he is pulling the handkerchief out of the box or your pocket and handing it to you after you sneeze.

You can see that this trick will take a bit longer than jumping through a hoop or "Aren't you ashamed of yourself?" Be patient and have fun with it—remember, this is just a game! If your dog picks it up quickly, that's great, but if he catches on more slowly, don't be discouraged! Think of this as a great way to occupy him during bad weather. Karen, who is from Los Angeles, never would have survived the worst of Wisconsin's winters if she hadn't been able to keep Bugsy, her much-loved but not-so-brilliant dog, occupied with trick training.

Sniffing on Cue

Here's the easiest trick in the world to teach your dog, because, like sit and down, your dog already knows how to do it. You just want her to do it on cue. You say "Sniff" and let your dog take a whiff of whatever you are pointing out. Granted, this trick isn't going to amaze your friends, but your dog will love it. Finally, she gets to smell all the objects in the house that she's never been able to lay a nose on! An extra benefit of this simple trick is that it can help your dog adjust to new things. It's great for dogs who are a bit hesitant of new objects or even unfamiliar people. Don't, however, ask your dog to sniff strangers if she has a history of stiffening or growling (much less biting) in that context. If that is the case, you'd be wise to find an experienced trainer or behaviorist to help you teach her a more appropriate response.

Get started by simply holding an object at nose level about three inches in front of your dog's face and saying "Sniff." Unless your dog is afraid, she'll sniff it automatically, because that's how dogs investigate their environment. You can try five or ten different items for each session, since virtually everything smells different to a dog. You can take out ten books from your bookshelf and be guaranteed that to your dog, each one has a unique smell. Dogs seem to love this game, and it's an incredibly easy way to entertain them. Eventually, she will associate the word "Sniff" with smelling something, and will inhale on cue to get a good whiff of any object.

You can graduate to lots variations on this trick, including asking your dog to sniff something at a distance away, or a specific object if he's learned the names of things. You could say "sniff your bed" or "sniff your ball" as a way to direct him around a space and keep him entertained while you watch television or make dinner.

Which Hand Has It?

Dogs are such smell-oriented creatures that teaching them to use their noses is often easier than teaching them most other things. Here's an easy trick that can be the basis for an entire magic show: Your dog uses her nose to determine which hand is holding a hidden treat.

To get started, put a strong-smelling treat in one fist so that it is showing a bit. Hold both fists down at the level of your dog's chest and ask, "Which hand?" If she shows any interest in the hand with the treat—sniffing at it, nosing at it, licking it, or pawing it—open your hand to let her get it. If she chooses the wrong hand, simply say, "Oops," open your hand to show her there's nothing there, and wait 30 to 60 seconds before trying again.

Keep doing this, washing the scent off your hands between each repetition to avoid confusing your dog, until she is good at choosing the correct hand. Make sure you vary which hand has the treat—lots of dogs have a tendency to choose the hand in which they last found the reward, and once a dog gets this in her head, it can be hard to change. When your dog is making the right choice reliably, start asking her to choose with the treat covered up a little bit more. Gradually cover more and more of the treat until your dog can make the right choice with it completely hidden. Then, she's ready to show off the trick to others!

It's extra charming if your dog indicates her choice by "pointing" at it with her paw. Once your dog will reliably use her nose to indicate the correct hand, try waiting up to five seconds after she makes her choice to see if she will use her paw rather than her muzzle. Many dogs will attempt to use their paw to get at the treat if they do not get it by poking their nose at it. This is more likely to happen if you hold the treat a bit lower than the level of her shoulders.

Besides being endearing on its own, this trick is one of the first steps towards teaching your dog a more advanced trick, the "Shell Game." In this game, you hide a treat under one of three cups, shuffle them around, and your dog uses her nose or paw to indicate where the treat ended up.

ORGANIZED CLASSES

There's a reason that organized sports are so popular. Besides being lots of fun, learning new skills in a group setting can provide support, motivation, and inspiration.[6] Many dogs seem to love the energy generated by a group, and if that describes your dog, we encourage you to find a class in your area that suits the two of you.

Keep in mind that not all dogs enjoy group classes. Some are nervous around other dogs, while some are uncomfortable around unfamiliar people or in areas with a lot of noise. If your dog shows signs of anxiety in group settings—yawning or lip licking, avoiding other dogs, barking continually (and of course, growling)—skip the group classes and play games at home. After all, play is supposed to be fun, not stressful! You might want to work with a trainer or behaviorist to ease your dog into such situations, but don't plunk a fearful dog down in the middle of a room full of barking strangers and expect him to "get over it." Tossing a dog into "the deep end" could teach him to swim, but more likely it will teach him to be terrified of water, and maybe even of you.

One last point about group classes: Be sure that the methods used are based on positive reinforcement. Beware of instructors who say they employ positive methods and then use leash corrections and prong collars, along with a little verbal praise. Positive reinforcement is defined by what your dog loves, and it's usually food, play, belly rubs, toys, or lots and lots of exuberant praise. It is NOT the pat-patting on top of the head in a way

---

6 And let's be honest—the odds are that at least one person is going to be worse than you are, which can be downright reinforcing for those of us who, like both authors, have spent entire softball games standing in right field thinking "Please don't hit the ball to me! Please don't hit the ball to me!"

that humans seem to enjoy and dogs hate, or giving them a dry, plant-based biscuit when what they want is a piece of meat or to play with the dog next to them. Well-run classes with instructors who know how to use positive reinforcement are so much fun for your dog that she should want to race through the door to get into the classroom. If she doesn't want to enter the training area, think long and hard about what's going on. A good instructor can provide invaluable advice in this case, and may advise a different type of class or playing games at home. That said, here is a list of the more common classes you can take with your dog, the games you'll learn in each, and a few comments about what kind of dogs (and people) enjoy them.

Agility

Agility is a team sport in which dog and owner move through an obstacle course that includes jumps, tunnels, see-saws, and weave poles. Some dogs absolutely adore agility, and it's tremendously fun to watch, even if your dog isn't the one performing. It's become a highly competitive sport in many countries; serious participants work for hours every day to shave tenths of a second off their time. However, you can play at any level—teaching your dog to hop over a few jumps in your backyard or joining a team and going for the gold. Once past the beginning level, dogs are off leash, and thus the sport requires a dog with training and impulse control. Part of why it is such fun for participants and spectators alike is that things can get pretty exciting, which means that dogs who don't handle arousal well aren't suited for the sport. Although it's the dogs who do the jumping and the weaving, the people need to be healthy enough to keep up with them—it's definitely not an activity for couch potatoes of either species! It also needs to be done with safety in mind; your dog could get hurt if she isn't trained correctly from the beginning or if she has any physical issues that could be exacerbated by this rigorous sport. Keeping those caveats in mind, agility can be the best thing that happens to some dogs, giving them confidence and a zest for life that is a joy to behold. You can learn more about agility at *www.cleanrun.com*.

Tracking

This activity allows dogs to use their natural abilities to follow the trail of a specific person or object. This is another game you can play just for fun or as a competitor, although you do need to learn something about the world of smell before you get started. We humans are often oblivious to smells, so we have to be very careful about how we teach dogs to follow a trail, lest we inadvertently mess up and compromise a scent trail that is undetectable to us. Thus, like agility, this is something you are best off learning from someone who knows the sport and how to teach it. Tracking is a wonderful way to spend time outside with your dog, especially if you would enjoy learning about the world of smells that is such a big part of your dog's life. It does involve a lot of exercise and carrying marker flags, maps of the track you laid, and other pieces of equipment, so organizational skills are very helpful here. Tracking can be wonderful for dogs who need a little confidence. There's nothing like teaching a dog to use her full range of skills—from nose work to athleticism—to bring out her inner wonder dog! Go to *www. workingdogweb.com/Dog-Sports-Tracking.htm* for more information.

Flyball

This is a sport that evolved from a game played casually in Southern California in the late 1960s. In flyball, two teams of dogs race side-by-side over a series of jumps, catch a tennis ball that flies out of a box when the dog presses a lever, and race back over the jumps. As soon as the first dog crosses the finish line, the next dog on the team takes his place, much like relay races in swimming or track. Dogs who like flyball are obsessed with retrieving, love speed and excitement, and are not put off by high-intensity energy. They also need to be in top physical condition. People who like flyball don't need to get any exercise at all, but their ears need to be immune to the din of barking dogs! It's an exciting, high-energy sport that is clearly great fun for the right participants, but it's not something that all dogs enjoy. To learn more, go to *www.flyballdogs.com*.

Mushing

No, this is not cuddling on the couch kissing your dog's furry face, although somewhere, someone could probably figure out how to make that a competitive sport. Mushing is the fancier's name for sled dog racing, although it technically refers to any kind of sport or transport that involves a dog pulling a sled, a cart, or you on skis for that matter (skijoring). This is a great way to exercise your dog, and a satisfying way to harness your dog's ability to haul you around the neighborhood. Obviously, this is not a game for all dogs—pugs and Chihuahuas aren't commonly seen in weight-pulling contests—but you don't have to have an Alaskan Malamute to participate, either. Healthy dogs, especially the kind who love to run, can have a wonderful time using their energy in a constructive way. Check out *www.dogplay.com/Activities/harness.html* for information on sled dogs, weight pulling, skijoring and more pulling-related activities.

Freestyle

Freststyle is a way to dance with your dog in a kind of choreographed performance set to music. The first time Patricia saw a freestyle exhibition performed by the deservedly famous Sandy Davis and her dog Pepper, tears came to her eyes. Imagine individuals of two species coordinating their movements to music, both having so much fun you can barely keep from tapping one on the shoulder and cutting in. Freestyle requires a dog who has strong focus and the drive to work as a team, one who is comfortable doing all kinds of silly things around his human (for instance, going through the person's legs, backwards). Like all the other organized games mentioned here, you can participate at any level, from dancing in your living room to competing in a national level competition. Find lots more information at *www.canine-freestyle.org*.

Herding

Yet another activity that will bring out your dog's inner canine, herding is a wonderful way to provide a dog with mental and physical exercise. The challenge with herding is that you need an actual herd to do it—it's a lot easier to put some agility equipment in your back yard than a flock of sheep. However, if you don't have your own livestock, you might be able to find someone close by who has animals who are used to being worked by dogs, and who can provide lessons for you and your dog. You do NOT want to work an inexperienced dog on livestock that has never been worked by a dog (and worked well, meaning gently). That would go as smoothly as putting an inexperienced rider on a horse who has never been ridden. Oh dear. Herding is exciting and challenging, but it also can be dangerous, so get lessons from someone you've learned to trust before you throw your dog in a pen with a bunch of huge, hoofed animals. A good source of herding information for all breeds is *www.stockdog.com*.

Obedience

Much more than having your dog come when called, "Obedience," as used in the dog fancy, refers to a set of precise exercises that are the basis for popular competitions that attract dog lovers all around the county. If done as a game with lots of positive reinforcement, obedience training and competitions can be great fun for dogs. High levels of obedience include in-depth communication between owner and dog, lots of precision (fractions of an inch count) and a marching-band kind of energy that can be quite engaging. Beware, though, of old-fashioned classes that use compulsion and punishment. Good obedience training is more like a game, not an exercise in domination and control. Spin-off classes include Rally which is a less formal version of obedience competition, and Canine Good Citizenship (CGC) classes that help dogs learn manners around unfamiliar people and dogs.

Tricks

Tricks are great fun to learn in a class setting. If you enjoyed the trick section in this booklet, look for a class near you. Teaching tricks is a wonderful way to learn the precision timing involved in clicker training, so you might want to double dip and look for a class that teaches tricks using clickers. Well-run trick classes are guaranteed to lift your spirits, no matter how hard a day you've had. Even when dogs (and people!) mess up, it's charming, and you'll get some ideas for tricks you'd never thought of on your own. Need a lift? Take two tricks classes and call us in the morning.

Games

Games classes allow you to play with your dog and other fun-loving people. Some common games include ones in which dogs compete at tic-tac-toe by holding their stays on a giant board and relay races that consist of standard obedience exercises and tricks at designated spots that each member of the team does individually. Games classes can include playing musical chairs, with each person "winning" a chair by sitting in it and then getting his/her dog to hold a down-stay. There's a board game often used in games classes called "My Dog Can Do That," which allows players to advance when their dogs perform actions such as touching their paw to their nose, walking around a chair, or retrieving an object. The best classes often include just-for-fun contests, such as whose dog can wag his entire body the most exuberantly—after all, it *is* a class about playing games and having fun! Dogs and people who like to try new things, are good sports no matter who wins a competition, are comfortable in the classroom even if gets a bit hectic, and are social with members of both species are likely to enjoy a games class. You might want to sit in on a local class to see if you think you and your dog would enjoy it; most dog training clubs and businesses would be glad to have you check them out for one night.

TOYS: THE GOOD, THE BAD, and THE SQUEAKY

Surely one of the reasons we get along so well with our dogs is our mutual love of "things," even when we're all grown up. Whether toys are tossed, chased, pounced upon, shaken, or torn into pieces, they are a wonderful bridge between individuals who speak different languages but want to play together. Toys also offer healthy ways to encourage our dogs to be creative, to solve problems, and to get in touch with their inner predator. There is no end to the many benefits of toys… but all toys are not created equal.

The Right Stuff

You've undoubtedly noticed that the market for dog toys has exploded in recent years. The availability of products like Dog Perignon Champagne plush toys, Hairy Winston squeak toys, and chewable Dolce and Grrrbana designer shoes gives you lots of choices—and a few headaches. If you want to experience sensory overload, go to a pet supply store or search online for "dog toys." Given all the choices, how do you decide what toys are right for you and your dog, and which toys are not?

Luckily, you have an expert in your house—your dog. All toys are not interesting to all dogs any more than they are to all people, so it's important to know what toys your dog likes. Some dogs like soft plush toys and others like bouncy toys made of durable rubber. Squeaky toys are value-added commodities in some households, and get no attention in others. Remember that your dog gets to say what he wants to play with—no matter how expensive the toy or how good the advertising copy, if he doesn't enjoy it, it's not worth the investment.

Take a few minutes to think about which toys your dog likes best. The most playful of dogs may like all kinds of toys, but they usually have favorites that you can use to make training more fun and effective. Sometimes it's useful to put away those special toys and only let your dog play with them during training sessions for a few weeks.

It's not a problem if your dog isn't toy crazy, but if so, it might be worth trying to encourage your dog's interest in objects. Some dogs learn to love toys after you give them hollow ones stuffed with food. A couple of weeks of licking frozen food out of a Kong® can work wonders. Rotating toys also helps keep your dog from getting bored—apparently the cliché "familiarity breeds contempt" applies to dogs, too. Keep three or four of your dog's toys out at any given time and store the others away. Every week or so, take some out and put others away, which provides novelty without requiring you to single-handedly support your neighborhood pet store. But again, don't despair if your dog is not interested in toys. Lots of other ways to play with your dog are described elsewhere in the booklet.

Since you can't send your dog out shopping (thank heavens), it's up to you to find toys that are safe, fun, and hardy enough to last longer than it takes to clip off the tag. It's a benefit if they are also not outrageously priced or so painful when stepped upon in the middle of the night that you lose your personal PG rating. A surprisingly small percentage of the many toys available actually meet all of the above requirements.

Safety First. Safety is the number-one issue, and unfortunately, many toys on the market have serious flaws that can make them dangerous. Many toys are made of lightweight plastic or flimsy rubber that are easily torn apart and could be swallowed, either choking your dog or causing an intestinal blockage. Rope toys and rawhide can also cause choking, which is why supervision is critical whenever your dog has his paws (or his mouth) on one of these.

The safest toys resist breaking into pieces, have no sharp edges, and are made out of the safest materials possible. Dogs who are strong chewers do best with round toys that are too big to be placed between the large molars—the teeth designed for crushing the leg bones of large ungulates (elk, for example)—at the back of their jaws. Toys should be too big to be swallowed, so make sure that the ones you give your dog are the correct size, and get rid of puppy-sized toys as he grows. If you are not sure that a toy is too small for your dog now, it probably is, so err on the side of caution and get it out of your house. Supervision can help, but can't always prevent trouble.

Size Matters, But So Do Materials. Some toys are made with ingredients that may not be healthy for our dogs. We all know that recalls for children's toys have become increasingly common, and surely it is optimistic to assume that our dogs' safety has been assured by those who manufacture canine toys. We urge you to adopt a "buyer beware" attitude, and to buy from companies that make their toys from safe—and ideally, recyclable—materials.

Duration, Duration, Duration. Another concern when choosing toys isn't so much about safety, but how long the toy will last. If a toy lasts no longer than a single play session, you need a compelling reason to buy it. Spending your paycheck on expensive stuffed toys that are ripped into shreds in minutes might not be the best use of your hard-earned money. However, sometimes the cost is justified. It might be worth the extra expense if a short-lived plush toy is the only way to keep your dog from going insane on Halloween. Other occasions to splurge on toys that will not last long are when your in-laws are visiting and your dog just HAS to be on his best behavior, when she is on "crate rest" for any reason[7], when you are treating her for a serious behavioral problem and need her absolute favorite toy for maximum effectiveness, or you want to give her (or yourself!) a special treat.

---

7 The phrase "crate rest" cannot be used without the addition of quotation marks by anyone who has been told to restrict her adolescent dog's movement for two months.

Laser Toys. One last word of caution, and then it's back to playing. Laser toys can engage dogs for hours, creating flashes of light that move around like crazed mice your dog can't quite ever manage to catch. They've also increased the client load of trainers and behaviorists all over the country by causing no small number of dogs to develop obsessive-compulsive-like behavior—staring at the wall for hours, waiting for a beam of sunlight to appear, or reacting so strongly to the shine of a car's headlights that they can't go on a walk anymore. Bottom line? It's not worth the risk.

You'd think, with all the cautions listed above, there'd be few toys left for you and your dog to play with. But there are hundreds of them—so many that there's not enough room in a small booklet to list all the good, amazing toys that are available now, not to mention the new ones that are being invented all the time. Here is a by-no-means inclusive list, designed to guide and inspire you.

TOYS FOR THROWING
(and for Your Dog to Bring Back!)

You can still throw a stick for your dog to fetch, but not everyone has a back yard full of sticks. In addition, not all dogs care much about them, and sticks can be dangerous and end up hurting your dog (oh, dear, here we go again!). Fetch games are better played with balls, flying discs, or any safe object that your dog loves enough to chase after and catch in his mouth.

Round Things That Roll

These have to be the most popular toy ever with both people and dogs. (Have you noticed that television news spends as much time on the fate of balls—tennis balls, basketballs, footballs, golf balls—as on world affairs?) The gold standard of fetching toys is the tennis ball, and rarely has there been a less expensive, versatile, good-for-us/good-for-them toy. The downside of tennis balls is that they turn slimy and soggy after just a few tosses, and dogs can wear down their teeth chewing off the fuzz. If the slimy ball bothers you, get a Chuckit!, a plastic tool that lets you scoop up and toss the ball without touching it.

But don't stop there. There are a plethora of round, rolling things in the world, and you just have to find your dog's favorite. Favorites at the McConnell house include the Orbee-Tuff® Orbee Ball and Strawberry Treat Spot (Get it? Sweet spot, treat spot?). West Paw Design's Huck, made of Zogoflex® , bounces, floats, and moves randomly, making it a delight for dogs who love to bat things around with their paws. As a bonus, these toys are made of ecofriendly materials and can even be recycled. For even more exciting games of fetch, try a Las Vegas version of a plain ol' ball—the blinking Fetch & Flash® ball.

Not all fetch toys have to be round. Ruff Dawg makes "The Stick," which is a rubber, stick-shaped toy that can't hurt your dog but is perfect for fetching. The folks at Kong® have a vast line of toys of all shapes covered in tennis ball-like fuzz for retrieving, tossing, and knocking around. You and your dog might also love Planet Dog's Slobber-Wick ™ Squeak Buddy. It's not plastic, it's not plush, but it's made of a fabric that somehow absorbs dog spit without getting slimy and gross. It's shaped like a gingerbread man, has a squeaker inside, and is tough enough to survive all but the most dedicated squeaker destroyer. Our canine tester experts loved it! (They also have squeakless versions, in case you or your pup has sensitive ears.)

There are at least a gazillion more possibilities out there and we can't begin to cover even a small percentage of them. It often takes some experimenting to find your dog's favorite, and you can always donate any rejects to your local shelter.

Disc-Shaped Toys

Some dogs love adding Olympic-style leaps to their fetch games, and if you do it safely, it can be fantastic exercise for your dog. It didn't take long after the Frisbee® came out for dogs to start getting in on the fun. Before long, an entire world of "disc dogs" developed, and now they have their own versions of the toy. Note that regular flying discs can injure a dog's teeth, so you definitely want to use discs specifically made for canines. These include the Chuckit! Flying Squirrel, the Fat Cat Hurl-A-Squirrel, and the Soft Bite Floppy Disc, which floats and has hot pink edges, making it easy to locate after an errant throw. (Notice the voice of experience here. Karen has found them under bushes, behind poles, and in trash piles, and has yet to lose one.) West Paw's Zisc™ is a soft, brightly colored disc that is easy to throw and seemingly indestructible. The Chewber Tug 'n Toss is a nice versatile variation—it can be used for tossing, tugging, and even as a water dish. After a hard year's use at Patricia's farm, it still looks like new; think of it as the Swiss Army Knife of dog toys.

A word of warning: Dogs aren't designed to throw themselves four feet into the air, twist around to catch something in their mouth, and then land as best they can. Ask your veterinarian if your dog is healthy enough for disc play, play on a flat surface, and don't expect your dog to do too much at any given time. All that having been said, dogs seem to love the challenge of catching something in mid-air as much as we like to watch them do it, so it's a great way to exercise your dog's mind and body at the same time.

TUG TOYS

Tug toys can be made out of a variety of materials, but need to be long enough to keep your dog's mouth at least two feet away from your hands. Even the best of dogs can get overexcited and end up biting your fingers instead of the toy. The least expensive tug toy is simply a thick knotted rope, but it might be just as easy for you to buy a commercially made toy at a pet store. A few popular toys include the Donkey Tail Tug Toy, Kong's® Tug Toy, and Tennis Tug. Flossy Chews® and Fleecy Cleans™ are long, stretchy braids made from materials said to help dogs clean their own teeth. They don't get as slimy as some tug toys, or as strongly scented with "eau de dog breath" either. Fire Hose toys are a line of dog toys that are actually made out of fire hoses, but we're told that lots of dogs other than Dalmatians enjoy them (sorry). These are not safe to leave out for big chewers to shred, but do make great tug toys for most dogs.

INDEPENDENT PLAY WITH PUZZLE TOYS

While this book is primarily about ways to play interactively with your dog, it is worth talking about toys that your dog can play with by himself. The primary purpose of dog toys may not be to give us a moment in which to read the paper or have a cup of coffee, but surely we've all used them that way! That's not a bad thing—it's good for dogs to learn to play by themselves. In addition, many toys can exercise a dog's mind and body without input from you. Puzzle toys keep dogs' brains (and paws and noses) occupied as they figure out how to get the treats you have hidden inside. Each one takes some combination of dexterity, reasoning, persistence, and sometimes a sense of smell to work out. The toys range in difficulty from canine kindergarten to rocket science for dogs.

There are many benefits to puzzle toys, including the fact that they provide mental stimulation, problem-solving practice, and a chance to increase dexterity and coordination, as well as the fun of succeeding at new challenges. After all, dogs are born problem solvers, and like all animals, working for their food is a natural part of their repertoire. Mental exercise is just as important as physical exercise, since many dogs suffer as much from boredom as from lack of activity.

The simplest puzzle toys have an interior space that can be stuffed with food, requiring your dog to chew, lick, and paw to get the food out. Dogs can spend enormous amounts of time removing the food, either by holding the toy with their paws and licking or by tossing it around so that food flies out of it. (Stuffing the toy with wet food and then freezing it can keep your dog busy for a *really* long time!) This is a great way to provide your dog with both food and mental and physical stimulation. It can also go a long way toward meeting your dog's daily requirement of "Hey! Life is interesting!" and it takes little effort from you. Sweet.

Stuffable toys can also teach formerly uninterested dogs to be engaged in object play, and that in itself makes them worthwhile. The granddaddy of hollow, stuffable toys is made by Kong®, in which we all should have bought stock fifteen years ago. Life without a Kong® is now hard to imagine—somewhat along the lines of life without duct tape or Post-it® notes. Kongs® are easy to stuff, shaped to fit dogs' mouths, and made out of the same indestructible rubber as airplane tires. Although Kong® is the best-known stuffable toy, it's not the only one. For variety or to experiment with which stuffable toy your dog loves best, try an Orbee-Tuff® Orbo, the Havaball®, Premier's football and an Orbee-Tuff® Bone.

Some toys, like the Roll-A-Treat ball and the Buster® Cube, require your dog to push and roll them over to cause pieces of food to fall out. The combination of an enthusiastic dog and a hard floor can result in noise levels reminiscent of a 747 about to take off, so you might want to pass on these if you are sound sensitive. The IQube™ and the IntelliBone™ are quieter but are also designed with canine higher education in mind. Dogs can spend hours happily playing with the removable parts, learning to use their mouths, paws, and noses to manipulate objects. Many dogs can remain engaged with these toys for a long time without any input from you. (However, some dogs get a kick out of you putting pieces together or hiding parts of the toy inside other parts of the toy.)

Other types of problem-solving toys have no hidden food, relying instead on those ever-enticing squeakies. Some dogs love little more than to rip and destroy the expensive toys we bring them from the pet store, so you might as well concede to their inner predator, and help them find ways to do it safely and within your budget. Some popular versions include Egg Babies, with removable squeaky eggs hidden inside, and the Jackpot Chipmunk, which has a Velcro® closure pocket containing a plush-covered squeaker. Booda Rip 'Ems are another kind of "if you can't beat 'em, join 'em" toy. The pieces of these toys are attached with Velcro®, and can be reattached in a variety of ways. Many dogs seem to love the ripping sound the Velcro® makes as much as the feeling of pulling the toy apart.

Perhaps the most sophisticated toys on the market right now are in the Zoo Active line, a family of top-quality wooden toys that require a dog to line up holes, slide parts around and spin things in order to make treats accessible. They've been popular in Europe for some time, and are now making a splash on this side of the Atlantic. They are expensive, but last a long time; they're also rare among puzzle toys in actually being attractive additions to your décor. The puzzles range in difficulty from The Dog Brick, which is pretty easy and a good starter puzzle for dogs, all the way up to The Twister, which is very challenging.

There are lots of other toys out there… we mention just a few to stimulate you to look around and to see what works best for you and your dog. Some dogs are happy with a few puzzle toys that they play with over and over, and other dogs seem to delight in having new ones to play with on a regular basis. Regardless, most dogs seem to like puzzle toys of one form or another.

Of course, most of these toys can do double duty as interactive toys. Karen's dog Bugsy, whom we've already described as a couple of ants short of a picnic, finally learned to fetch with a Jackpot Chipmunk. He dutifully brought the toy, which he could never figure out how to open, back to her so that he could be paid in liver biscotti for his hard work.

We know that as soon as we write any recommendations for toys, they will be out of date, because new dog toys come out all the time. We can't do much about this except to urge you to keep your feelers out for new and better toys. It wasn't that long ago that dog toys consisted of sticks and tennis balls, so celebrate the variety available while trying to stay within a reasonable budget. Keep checking on the companies that make your favorite toys—chances are they'll have some wonderful new ones for you soon.

PLAY YOUR WAY TO AN OBEDIENT DOG

Surely one of life's greatest joys is calling your dog to come and watching her turn on a dime and run toward you with a joyful expression on her furry face. It's wonderful to have a well-behaved dog who does what you ask whenever you ask it. One of the best ways to achieve that is to combine training and play, so that "obedience" becomes an enjoyable game that you and your dog play together. Games are great educational tools, and it's a lot easier to learn when you're having fun. We all know how different it feels to learn the rules of a game we love versus having something involuntarily drilled into our heads! Play is a powerful motivator to dogs, too, sometimes more powerful than anything else we can provide for them. Bomb- and narcotic-detection dogs are often trained with play as reinforcement, because their trainers have learned that play is more effective than food in that context. The wonderful irony of play is that you can use its light-hearted exuberance to teach your dog serious skills.

We're not sure which aspect of using play to teach obedience is better—the fact that it's fun or the fact that it works so well. And what a refreshing change from the perspective that says "You must sit when I say sit because you respect me as your alpha pack leader." We say alpha-schmalpha to that: We know of no social species in which a subordinate member is told to sit or lie down on cue. Moreover, who wants a dog who does what we ask because he is afraid not to obey?

We want our dogs to listen and respond to us because they've learned it's fun to do so. That's where play comes in. You can use play to help a dog understand what it is you want; to pay attention to you even when he's distracted; and, most importantly, to assist you in teaching your dog manners without compromising your relationship with him.

Play and "obedience" go hand and hand if you think about it. The games our children play all have rules, and learning to play requires that participants learn the rules and abide by them while they are having fun. Watch young children playing baseball for the first time—some will run to first base without hitting the ball, and then run triumphantly to home plate while everyone laughs and yells "No, no! You have to run to second base first!" Puppies start playing the same way, with little understanding of the rules of social engagement—they bite your hair and grab the remote control off the table and try to play soccer with it. But puppies and children all come with an innate understanding that games have rules, and accept learning them from their elders and their peers.

That means that standard "obedience commands" (doesn't that sound old-fashioned now?) like "sit" and "down" and "heel" can be interwoven into play in a way that makes following the rules part of the fun. With a light-hearted attitude, and by using play as a joyful reinforcement, you can end up with a dog who is sufficiently well trained to be the star of her own movie.

As we said earlier, play only works as reinforcement if your dog really loves doing it, so you need to know what kind of play makes your dog happy before you start. At the same time, don't hesitate to experiment and try to expand your dog's play repertoire, because it's best to have more than one way to play with your dog. Keep in mind that what makes play so effective is that it allows you to successfully vie for your dog's attention despite all the other exciting things in the environment. Let's face it—it's hard to be more interesting than the sight of another dog walking by the house, or the scent of a squirrel in the grass. Games give you the power to motivate your dog to pay attention to you—because you are literally the best game in town.

You'd also be wise to decide which exercises you want to focus on at any given time. It is better to teach your dog to excel at responding to a small number of cues rather than having a long list of them that only work part of the time. Before you continue, think for a moment what two or three behaviors you most want your dog to master, whether it's coming when called or walking politely on a leash.

A Word About Food

Our focus on play doesn't mean that we aren't in favor of using food as a reinforcement. Food is great, no question about it. Besides adoring it ourselves, we use it extensively in training. Food is a perfect attention-getter and a great way to reinforce a dog for doing what was asked. We would never suggest taking food off your list of tools when training your dog, but neither do we want you to limit yourself to using it as your only reinforcement, as so many people seem to do. It's best to use play as an addition to food reinforcements for several reasons. First, we all want our dogs to respond when asked, no matter what the context. The best way to do that is to provide a variety of reinforcements so that your dog learns that she feels good in a general sense if she complies. Just like us, dogs don't always want the same thing—if you mix and match food, praise, belly rubs, and play, she'll learn to respond whether she's hungry or not.

Sometimes play is a more powerful reinforcement than food. Say, for example, that your dog is a little nervous when she sees another dog down the block. Sometimes it works wonders to teach her that an approaching dog is a predictor of some wonderful food— "Oh boy, an approaching dog means I'm getting chicken! I love chicken! Chicken chicken chicken! I guess I love other dogs!" It's a method that has helped thousands of dogs in the past. However, some dogs will snatch the food from your hand but remain fearful or nervous. Other dogs are just plain uninterested in food. In these types of cases, play is more likely to elicit positive emotions. Those playful and relaxed emotions can transfer more easily to the sight of approaching dogs, and can lead to a dog who associates other dogs with feelings of happiness.

The next section suggests a few ways to incorporate play into some of the most common things we ask our dogs to do—come when called, be polite to visitors at the door, walk politely down the street with us, and sit or lie down when asked. We do not elaborate on the details of how to teach a recall or how to train a dog to heel; rather, we focus on ways to maximize the use of play to have a responsive dog. (See the Resources section for books on teaching general obedience from a positive perspective.)

Coming When Called and the Chase Game

Someday, perhaps someone will breed a dog who comes hard-wired with an automatic "come-when-called" gene, but we're not holding our breath. Recalls should be thought of as circus tricks, because it is not in the nature of a dog to stop what he is doing and instantly dash toward you just because you made a little noise in your throat (or even a big one!). Here's where a chase game comes to the rescue—it's the perfect way to teach a dog that coming when called is truly worth it, because he's learned that when you call "Come," he gets to run run run, and that is fun fun fun!

All you need to do is to say your dog's come signal before you turn and run away. Say "Chief! Come!" and then dash away from him, clapping, and—if you're into it—laughing as you run. You don't have to run far (thank goodness), just enough so that it feels like a game to your dog. You've already reinforced your dog for turning and moving toward you by letting him chase you, but you'd be wise to sweeten the pot by giving him a treat when he gets to you, or taking off in another direction to give him an opportunity for another chase. It will be more fun, and therefore more effective, if the game is unpredictable, so don't get in the habit of letting your dog run to you once and then ending the game. Do remember our cautions about stopping and turning to face your dog before he actually catches up, and don't let young children play this training game; it's just not safe for them.

How you position your body is going to have a big effect on your dog's behavior. If you stand squarely facing your dog and move toward him while you call "Come," you are going to inhibit him from moving toward you. Dogs want to go in the direction that your feet are going, so when you call your dog to come, turn your body sideways and move away from your dog as you call. Remember, it's a chase game, and you can't be chased if you're not moving away. This movement away will draw your dog toward you rather than blocking him from moving forward. You'll have to concentrate on this at first; it's not natural to turn your body and move away from your dog as you call him to come, but the pay-off is well worth the time and effort.

Avoid asking your dog to sit when he gets to you and only then reinforcing him—if you do, you're reinforcing the sit, not the coming when called. Sometimes it's fine to ask for a sit, but don't do it too much—it can make coming when called a bit of a drag! Also, guard against doing something that your dog *doesn't* like. For example, dogs love petting, but they usually aren't fond of pats on the crown of their head, and they are especially unwelcome during play sessions. (We envision them saying, like little boys on a playground whose mother has hugged them in front of their buddies, "Aw, M-o- o-o-o-o-m!")

Try playing this chase game several times a day, being sure to use your come signal immediately before your dog turns to run to you. (Did we mention the importance of saying it the same way every time? "Come" is not the same "C'mon" or "C'mere," and changing cues just makes things confusing to your dog.). Gradually, you can start calling your dog to come without having to hoof it across the lawn yourself every time. Start by running only a few steps away, then change to merely turning your body sideways as though *about to run* away. Eventually, you can say "Come" without having to move and your dog will start running toward you.

Continue to use chase games, treats, or anything special like a new toy to reinforce your dog for difficult recalls, keeping in mind that all recalls are difficult when a dog is immersed in a great set of smells or any riveting distraction. Imagine being on the last page of a mystery novel when someone calls you to come sit down to dinner! What would it take to put the book down with only one sentence to go?

Combined with food and other types of play (perhaps a game of tug when your dog gets to you after you call?), chase games can be amazingly effective at teaching a good recall. Of course, every dog is different, and some are easy to teach to come when called and some are, umm, more challenging. Some dogs will never be 100 percent trustworthy off leash in a distracting environment, and that's okay. Your job is to be aware of your dog's ability to control his impulses and his ability to make mature decisions. Know what most distracts him, and therefore, when you're better off going to get him and fetching him yourself rather than calling him to come. However, if you remember to make coming when called a great game to your dog, your dog will repay you for your efforts time and time again.

Tricks for Treats—Teaching Sit and Down with Tricks

Tricks are great fun to teach to your dog and to show off to visitors, but they can have another function as well. Given how much fun they are to teach and perform, why not use the tricks themselves as reinforcements for more mundane things, like sit and down? What if lying down on cue is all part of a game? What if sitting when asked means the fun has just begun? Not only does this make compliance fun for your dog, it can create a dog who is happy to sit or down when he's excited and aroused—which is when you need it most. It's easy to teach a dog to sit in the kitchen when he's quiet and calm and there's nothing else going on. However, getting a dog to sit or down when he's excited is another thing altogether. You can use the excitement of any kind of play as both reinforcement and a distraction if it's done thoughtfully. If you do, you'll have a dog who is used to listening and complying when he's feeling revved up, whether as a result of spotting a deer or playing with another dog.

Try teaching your dog that sit and down are predictors of a trick training session. Don't belabor it—just one or two sits or downs are enough. Guard against establishing a pattern—a sit, then a down and then the same trick, for example. Mix and match what you ask for, and be sure to do it in different places at different times of the day. Your dog will be much more responsive if you ask for one "surprise" sit in the hallway, followed by one quick trick and then a dash to the living room. So often we teach "obedience" in the same pattern in the same place, and then are surprised that our dog doesn't respond in a different context. That's one of the secrets that professional dog trainers learn early on—the importance of training out of a pattern and in different contexts. It's relatively easy to get into the habit—try scattering a "Bugsy, sit!" or a "Brodie, down!" when it's least expected, and following it up with his favorite trick. Of course, you can use any type of play to reinforce a sit or a down—wise owners use what their dogs like best, whether it's jumping through a hoop or playing tug. Once you do, you'll be amazed how quickly your dog learns to be responsive when it matters most.

Crazy Owners, Polite Dogs on Neighborhood Walks

Walking side-by-side with us is one of the hardest things we ask our dogs to do. We think it's trivial to stroll shoulder-to-shoulder, because that's how we automatically walk with our human friends. However, to a dog, heeling means "walk unnaturally slowly and ignore everything interesting." And we're surprised they don't do it on their own? Walking side-by-side isn't in a dog's natural repertoire—dogs don't walk beside each other when they're out and about, they scamper here and there and meet up with their friends over interesting smells in the grass.

Asking a dog to stay in a heel position, or at least not to haul you down the sidewalk like a sled across the Arctic, means that you are asking for your dog's attention the entire time you are walking. That's a lot to ask of an animal who is drawn to the smell of chipmunks under the hedge, and evidence of other dogs in the grass. This is why a playful attitude is so important when teaching a dog to walk politely on a leash. It inherently makes no sense to them, but if they think it's a game, they are much more likely to play by the rules. Here's how you can incorporate the "Crazy Owner" game, along with some good basic heel training (see the training books in the Resources section) to make walking your dog much more fun.

To review, we call it the "Crazy Owner Game," because it might provoke your neighbors to look out their windows and exchange worried glances. Rather than walking around the neighborhood straight down the sidewalk like a normal person, you zig and zag, speed up and slow down, moving erratically so that your dog has to pay attention to unpredictable you!

It's easy to incorporate the game into teaching a polite heel. Imagine you've said "Heel" and walked forward two steps. Your dog kept up with you, so you praise and give him a treat. (Don't even think about trying to teach heel without the liberal use of treats!) Now, stride forward for five steps, but take quick, little steps. Stop and praise effusively, then turn right and take two slow, big steps. Stop, treat, and praise. Start again, but this time go forward fast for five or six strides, then without stopping, turn right and slow down again, then turn 90 degrees to the left in front of your dog, take two more steps and release your dog. Now, stop and wave cheerfully to the person staring at you from across the street, then begin another round.

Give your dog lots of treats when he is in the heel position and the leash is loose so that he is interested and motivated to stay by your side. Heeling is one of the exercises that most requires an upbeat manner from the trainer, so start out with the animation level you'd have if you were about to perform the jitterbug on *Dancing with the Stars*. Remember, don't expect your dog to be upbeat and to pay attention if you're not doing the same!

Keep your heeling sessions short; it's not fair to expect a dog to pay such close attention for too long when you're getting started. (Try it yourself; walk beside someone who is moving briskly and try to stay exactly side-by-side with him. It's amazingly difficult, even for primates like us who normally walk beside one another.) What's most important is to remember what you are asking of your dog: to pay attention to you in the midst of a world full of interesting things. You are competing for your dog's attention, and you have a much better chance of getting and keeping it if you are truly someone worth watching—and if you don't ask for it for too long.

Avoid the most common mistake of novice trainers: forgetting to release the dog from a heel. If you aren't clear about when your dog is supposed to be heeling and when he is not, he will never know what you expect, and will start ignoring the heel cue when he feels like it. Remember, it takes a lot of energy for your dog to pay such close attention to you, and you simply can't expect him to do it ad infinitum. Underline this section; it is the hardest part of teaching a good heel, and one of the biggest differences between professional dog trainers and dog owners in general. When you release him, be sure to use the same cue every time, whether it's "okay" or "free" or another word that works for you. Avoid using a word that you say in other contexts. Now let your dog be a dog, and "read" the canine newspaper with his nose! You can avoid having him pull you when not on heel by using good equipment, either a head collar or a body harness with a chest-oriented leash attachment. Then both of you can enjoy your walk equally.

Polite Greetings at the Door and
Go Find Your Toy

Do you dread the idea of anyone ringing the doorbell, because when visitors come, your dog is so out of control it's embarrassing? If so, you're not alone—it's a rare dog owner who hasn't had trouble with a dog being too rambunctious at the door. You can't blame the dogs—a polite greeting in their society includes licking the sides of another's mouth. It's not their fault they have to leap into the air to connect with our muzzles. However, we can't blame our guests for being put off either; it's no fun to have someone else's dog launch himself like a rocket into your face. Here's another time that play can be your ally. You can use play to channel your dog's energy in a more appropriate direction and avoid unwanted drama at the door. The general idea is that, instead of filling the doorway with leaps, spins, and a cacophony of barking, you teach your dog to go get a toy.

Start by putting out some toys that your dog loves to carry around, whether they are plush or bouncy. Hollow toys filled with food can be especially useful, because your dog can settle down with them in the living room while you chat with your guests, and they work whether your dog is toy-oriented or not. (Note: Please don't do this if your dog is possessive over food.) Now, go to the door and *pretend* that you have company. Don't try to train your dog when real company arrives, a time when she can barely connect two neurons inside her furry little head. Rather, knock on the door yourself, or ring the bell, to simulate visitors. You can even use your "visitor voice" (trust us, you have one, and your dog knows it well) as you open the door. As soon as your dog goes into "visitor mode," encourage her to run to the room with the toys in it. You might want to start with a toy in your hand, and use it as a lure to get her away from the door. Once you get a good distance away from the door, encourage your dog to play with the toy, tossing it in the air, playing a fetch game with it, or showing her the treats hidden inside if it's a stuffable toy. After she's had a good time for two to three minutes, take the toy away, wait a few more minutes, and then pretend to have visitors all over again.

Your goal is to teach your dog to run away from the door and away from the visitors, and get a toy from another room. If your dog is super-friendly and über-exuberant, you can use this same technique to get her into a crate, where you give her a toy stuffed with food and let her chew on it until the excitement of the greeting is over. You can let her out after your guests have been in the house for about ten minutes, by which time things will have naturally calmed down. Toy-oriented dogs can quickly learn to respond to visitors by running to fetch a toy to show off to the newcomers. They'll be less likely to leap and bark if they've got a great big toy in their mouth.

Redirecting your dog to a toy when visitors come seems so simple, but sometimes simple is best. Dogs are easily over stimulated while greeting visitors at the doorway, so taking the dog out of the situation can make having visitors over a lot more fun. Even dogs who will sit when your guests enter can return to Olympic-quality high jumps after the first sit, or second, or for that matter, the third. So, if asking your dog to sit at the door isn't working for you, try redirecting her to a toy whenever anyone walks into the house (this includes you!) and you'll find that it can be a lot more fun to have company come over.

Tug and Teaching "Take It/Drop It"

Every dog gets something in her mouth that she shouldn't have, or holds onto a toy that you need to take back. You can get the object back by quietly saying "Drop it," which she's learned as an enjoyable game, or you can chase her around the yard, wrestle her to the ground, and pry open her mouth. Your choice. (The latter is not recommended.) Tug games are a great opportunity to fight fire with fire, and to teach your dog that if she drops something when you ask her to, she'll get to play a game that lets her pick it up again, and have a great time doing it. Thus, teaching tug can do double duty, both as a game you can use to entertain your dog and as a way of getting her to let go of something in her mouth.

Getting Started. Pick out a suitable tug toy and wave the end of the toy one or two feet in front of your dog's face. Just as she starts to open her mouth to take the toy, say "Take it." Remember to not pull back hard right away; let her get a good grip on it first, but once she has, pull back steadily to encourage her to tug against you. Praise your dog while she's tugging, and pull back hard enough to stimulate her to match your effort. If she drops the toy, shake it a few feet in front of her to encourage her to pick it up again. Once she does, don't pull back until she's got a good grip on it again.

Take It/Drop It. Get your dog's favorite tug toy and a bag of small tasty treats. Put one of the treats in your non-dominant hand or a pocket, and start playing a rousing game of tug with the words "Take it!" After you've played for a minute, hold the toy with one hand and move the treat toward her nose with the other. Once the treat is only an inch or two from her nose, say "Drop it."

If the treat is good enough, and your dog loves food, she'll spit out the toy and take the food. As she does, praise her generously, saying "Good dog" enthusiastically. If your dog really loves tug, you can offer her the toy again, play another tug game, and repeat the sequence as above. However, some dogs are so food-motivated that they ignore the toy and look for more treats. If that happens, it's okay; just stop the game for a few minutes. You can also entice her into dropping the toy in her mouth by waving a second toy—just be sure that both objects are equally attractive to your dog. Exactly which two items you use varies from dog to dog—what matters is that your dog learns the fun doesn't stop when she opens her mouth after you say "Drop it,"

Your goal is to teach your dog that "Drop it" is just the flip side of "Take it." That way, she thinks of it as part of a game rather than a threatening command from an owner who wants to take her treasure away. During the first month or so of training, don't ask for a "Drop it" without having started with a "Take it." Play the Take It/Drop It game with her tug toy several times a day, always making her glad she dropped the object when you asked her to, and always keeping the mood light and playful. After a week or two, start asking her to play Take It/Drop It with any of her toys, always being ready with a favorite toy or tasty treat to make it worthwhile for her to give you the object when you say "Drop it." Eventually, you will have a dog who will drop anything at a quiet word from you, but understand that there is a lot of practice between getting started and expecting a dog to drop her favorite toy (or a hamburger wrapper) just because you ask her for it.

Using Tug Games to Teach Your Dog To Chill

Besides its other benefits, playing tug is a good way to teach dogs emotional control. Tug games can be highly stimulating, which is part of the reason they are so much fun for your dog. You can harness that energy under controlled conditions to teach your dog to calm down when you ask.

Of course, the flip side of that is that dogs can become too excited when playing tug, so it's important to avoid letting your dog become overly aroused when you're playing this game. If this might be an issue with your dog, be sure to read the section on page 79 titled "Know The Signs of Over Arousal." We also advise that you don't let pre-teen or younger children play tug with a dog. As we said above, tug can be highly stimulating, and it's a lot to ask a child to keep her own emotions under control, much less monitor those of the dog.

To teach a dog to calm down on cue, start by playing vigorously for a few seconds, and then do two things: Say "Chill" and stop all motion. Stop pulling back, stop moving around, and face your dog with a relaxed body and a neutral expression on your face. Dogs do this all the time when they are playing with one another; they'll play hard and then one of them will stop abruptly and go still while facing the other dog. In other circumstances it could look intimidating, but in the context of play, it seems to be taken as a "time out" signal. You can use this natural behavior to help your dog learn to "Chill" on cue. Keep your pauses very short; one second is long enough. If you stay still for too long your dog may begin to wonder if you are threatening her, so think of these pauses as though you were dancing: Stop for the count of one beat, and then continue waltzing across the floor.

Of course, when you pause, your dog will probably keep pulling back, but try to finesse your response by staying still, holding onto the toy, but not pulling back yourself. Most dogs catch on surprisingly fast, especially when you change from an engaged play partner to a statue. As soon as your dog pauses in the slightest way, say "Okay" and resume play as before. You can scatter two or three of these in a play session to get your dog used to pausing when she hears you say the word. After a few weeks, you can occasionally say "Chill," praise her if she stops pulling, and either resume play or end the game there.

At the same time, start using the word "Chill" in other contexts, being sure to ask when she has a good chance of getting it right. Reinforce her in whatever way is appropriate, even giving her a toy stuffed with food as a reward for settling down. Remember also that emotions and energy are contagious—if you want her to calm down, you need to move slowly, breathe deeply, and keep your voice measured and calm. As soon as you can do that under any circumstances—say, there are seven people at the door, the phone is ringing, the peas are burning, and your dog is throwing herself at your visitors—let us know. We'd like to invite you over.

Using Play for Any Other Training Exercise

You can use play for almost all the exercises you'd like your dog to perform. There isn't room to list them all here, but you get the idea—use appropriate types of play to motivate and teach your dog to listen and respond. There are several other cues we think are so important we suggest that everyone consider adding them to their repertoire. "Leave it" means turn away from whatever it is your dog is about to sniff or eat, "Wait" means please pause for a moment (and don't charge out of the car or the house the microsecond I open the door), and "This way" asks your dog to turn on a dime and move away from a potential problem (used most memorably when Karen and Bugsy ran into a coyote on a neighborhood walk).

Of course, the sky is the limit; there are so many ways you can make your dog glad to do what you ask. Using play is a wonderful way to get your dog to work with you instead of trying to figure out ways to beat the system. However, there are a few exceptions to using play to teach something new, and "Stay" is an important one.

Even though we love using play to reinforce polite behavior, play is not appropriate for every exercise. Stay is a perfect example, because the early stages of good stay training teach a dog that the fun is in staying put, not in getting up. For decades, dog trainers did it the other way around—telling dogs to stay in place until released, and only then reinforcing them with food, play or praise. If you think about it, that's backward! We want our dogs to *want* to stay in place when asked, not to quiver with excitement in anticipation of the release. That's why we teach stay by giving our dogs treats while they are holding their stays. You could call it the "good things come to those who wait" method, and it results in dogs who don't even want to get up when you release them. (This is a high-quality problem indeed.) It's almost impossible to use play to reinforce a dog during a stay without causing them to get up, so use treats while the dog is on stay and keep the release boring.

Integrating Stay and Play

Although you can't use play to teach a dog the initial phases of a stay, it's a great idea to intersperse stay within a play session. In this way, you can teach your dog emotional control and help him learn to listen even when he's excited. Here's an example from Patricia's farm. Her two Border

Collies love to play fetch games, but the young one, Will, can outrun the older one, Lassie, every time. To ensure that Lassie gets to play too, Patricia asks Will to lie down and stay a few times while she throws the toy for Lassie. You can imagine that this was very hard for young Will at first—stay lying down and watch another dog run after the flying disc? Patricia got it started step-by-step, by asking for a stay of only a second while she stood right beside him and tossed the disc just a few feet toward Lassie. If Will held his stay for as little as one second, he got another toy to fetch himself. Gradually, she asked for longer stays, and worked up to throwing Lassie a good, long toss while Will stayed in place. As soon as Will was released, he got to chase the disc himself, and he now accepts that an occasional stay is just part of the fetch game. He's learned a lot about controlling his own emotions even when he's highly motivated to do something else. This "on-off" button will be invaluable (and potentially life-saving) in many situations in the future, from herding sheep to paying attention when a deer shows up across the road.

YOU DON'T ALWAYS HAVE TO PLAY

Most dogs would love to spend the day doing nothing but playing and sleeping, but then, so would we. If you've figured out how to do that and still earn enough money to buy dog food, please let us know. However, you probably have a few other things to do—like go to work, make dinner, or read the paper. Playing with your dog may be part of what makes your life complete, but it should not be your life completely. Part of being a good play partner is communicating clearly when it's time to play, and when it's not.

It might seem ironic that a booklet encouraging you to play with your dog is also advising that you don't become a slave to your dog's demands to play, even if he spends most of the day in a crate while you are at work. Yes, your dog needs lots of physical and mental exercise, but that doesn't mean it's okay for him to pester you relentlessly all evening long. You and your dog will be much happier in the long run if you are clear about when you are ready to play and when you're not. That way, you are both willing participants in the game, which makes it a lot more fun. Besides, being at your dog's beck and call is not a kindness to anyone. It's bad for you, and can pollute the
relationship you have with your dog, making you less likely to play another time. It's bad for your dog because it keeps him in a semi-aroused state all evening ("Are we going to play or not? Maybe if I just keep pawing/barking long enough..."), rather than being able to predict and understand what's going on around him. Dogs who get reinforced for constantly badgering their owners can lose their ability to tolerate frustration and become emotionally aroused in ways that don't serve themselves or anyone else.

There are undoubtedly some people reading this section whose dogs have never pestered them to play. Their Greyhound or Akita is lying quietly beside them, and is no more likely to solicit play than to clip his own nails. The least that those lucky people can do is to have sympathy for people whose dogs throw toys in their laps, bark through the best part of the movie they're watching, or stare at them as if they were dairy cows on the way to the barn for milking. Dogs who never initiate play probably need their owners to do it for them, but the rest of us are wise to have a signal that says "Not now!"

Teaching "Enough"

(Or, I'm Sorry, Your Human Is Not Available to Play Right Now.)

Luckily for us, dogs have a social signal that, translated from canine, means "I'm not available for social interaction right now." This useful canine signal is descriptively called a "look away," and can be incorporated into a cue called "Enough." The best part about this cue is that it's easy to teach, and dogs understand it amazingly fast in many different contexts.

Sitting on your couch or comfy chair, start by saying " Enough" in a low, quiet voice and then patting your dog briskly on the head two times.[8] Most dogs are not fond of pats on top of the head (do it to yourself—it feels lousy) and some of them will walk away without further ado. However, most dogs won't give up right away, especially young, energetic types and those who have not had a lot of boundaries set for them in the past.

In this case, stand up and move your dog a few feet away from the chair, using your legs to back him away. Don't push him away with your hands (that can be misinterpreted as play) or pick up your feet and try to shove your dog backwards with them. Stay silent, keep your feet on the ground, and quietly shuffle forward a step or two between your dog and your chair.

---

8 We're not talking about petting here, which most dogs adore, we're talking about two brisk pats on top of the dog's head. Unless a dog is hand-shy, they aren't frightened by it, but they aren't fond of it either. Patricia's nieces call them "happy slappies," a good reminder that they should be done with the most cheerful of intentions!

As you inch forward, your dog will most likely respond by backing up or by trying to go around you to the left or right.

If your dog tries to go around you, your job is to act like a goalkeeper and move right or left to counter your dog's attempts to get around you and back toward the chair. Stay quiet and calm, imagining that you are protecting a small area of space rather than trying to force your dog into anything. Once your dog has moved back a step or two (don't expect too much), sit back down, cross your arms and *turn your head up and away from your dog* as he moves back toward you.

This is the "look away" part of the signal, and dogs seem to understand it instantly. All you have to do is turn your head so that your face is pointed away from your dog, and point your chin upward. Most dogs respond by walking away and looking elsewhere for something to do, or someone else to do it with. Don't make the oh-so-common mistake of telling your dog to go away, and yet continuing to make eye contact with him. If you keep staring at him, saying things like "Not now," or "Go lie down," he'll keep staring back, trying to figure out what you want. If you turn your face away, arms folded, you are clearly communicating that you don't want to interact right now.

Although crossing your arms is not technically part of a look away (we've never seen dogs do it!), it can be useful to add it to your repertoire as you look away. Crossing your arms presents a "closed" rather than an "open" body posture, and most importantly, keeps you from reaching for the dog, especially if it's to push him away. Dogs often bat at each other with their paws during play, so this action is easily misinterpreted, and conveys the exact opposite of what you are trying to communicate.

Persistent dogs, bless their hearts, may respond to a look away by coming around to the side you're facing and trying again to get your attention. Just keep your arms folded and turn your face up and away from your dog again. Sometimes it takes three or more head turns, and maybe another set of brisk pats to the head to deter enthusiastic dogs, especially if they are accustomed to getting your attention whenever they want. Don't worry— adult dogs commonly give multiple look aways when puppies are pestering them, and the message eventually gets across.

One of the keys to getting this to work right away (you can train some dogs to walk away to the verbal cue "Enough" in one or two trials—it's almost scary!) is to work on being committed to the message. Subtlety is counter-productive when trying to communicate across species, so pretend you're an actor and throw yourself into your role. If you need a role model, think of adolescent girls at their worst, who can be masters at dramatically turning their heads up and away while saying "I'm *not* talking to you!" Nobody can fault their clarity and accuse them of sending an ambiguous message.

We are *not* saying that you shouldn't give your dog attention. What's the fun of having a dog if you can't stop what you're doing and give her a belly rub, or let her remind you that the bills can wait—it's time to GET OUTSIDE AND PLAY! Just don't let your dog learn that she can get what she wants, whenever she wants it, just by demanding that you do what she wants RIGHT NOW! If you have a young dog who clearly needs attention or exercise, but you just have to finish the email you're writing, say "Enough" if she scratches at your leg (or whatever her version of making demands is), pat-pat her on top of the head, and look away. But once she gives up and settles herself down, get up yourself (stay quiet, no need to talk) and give her a toy stuffed with treats that you have cleverly stored in the freezer for this very moment. Give it to her in the same place in which she had settled in the first place, even if she's gotten up to follow you out of the room.

You can then go back to finishing your email, and your dog is happily engaged with something besides you. Most importantly, she's learned that it pays to settle down on the floor rather than working you like a slot machine. This is especially helpful for young dogs who can barely contain themselves. It's the equivalent of giving a young child a coloring book and crayons at a restaurant while you finish your meal—why not make life easier for everyone? There's nothing wrong with keeping everyone happily engaged until it's time to interact again.

HOW NOT TO PLAY WITH YOUR DOG

At the risk of sounding like the Play Police, we have lots to say about how *not* to play with your dog. We've seen too many broken-hearted owners whose dogs got in serious trouble because of inappropriate play. Remember when we said play is serious stuff? It is—dogs can die, and people can get badly hurt, all because someone played with a puppy in a way that caused trouble down the road. The advice that follows is based on our combined thirty years of experience working with people and dogs, and it's meant with the best of intentions. We absolutely want you to have a ball playing with your dog (just don't *be* the ball!).

Your Body is Not a Toy

It's not a good idea to let your dog play by biting or mouthing your arm or hand, no matter how gently. It's true that some dogs have done this all their lives and have never gotten in trouble because of it. Perhaps you have known a dog who always played like that and never hurt a play partner. That's great, but unfortunately, trainers and behaviorists see the other side all too often—dogs who hurt someone, sometimes badly, in the middle of a play session.

Here's the basis of the problem: The best part of play is the feeling of joyful abandon that often accompanies it. Frolicsome play allows us to shed some of our inhibitions—that's one of the reasons it's so good for us. We get to connect back to our inner child (possibly even find our inner puppy) and experience the innocent abandon of youth. Pure and simple, play is exciting, and that's why it's so much fun.

However, excitement is a kind of emotional arousal, and as exhilarating as it is, a little too much arousal can lead to trouble. That's true of any species that can get worked up, including our own. Emotional arousal in people is what turns hockey games into boxing matches, and soccer games into riots. Surely it is unrealistic to expect our dogs to exhibit more emotional control than we do!

Dogs who are highly aroused are not as good at controlling their own behavior as they are when they're not revved up. Aroused dogs get mouthier, and many of their actions become more vigorous. Play actions like mouthing, leaping, and body-slamming can cause a lot of harm if done too vigorously. Furthermore, they can frighten or overwhelm a play partner.

Dogs who play by biting at hands and arms are all too likely to bite too hard when the play gets overly arousing. Sometimes these bites are truly accidental, and sometimes they are the result of a dog who has lost her temper and bitten out of anger or frustration. Playground fights aren't restricted to elementary schools—it's not uncommon for dogs at a dog park to escalate from excitement to irritation, and from irritation to aggression. Smart owners supervise dog-dog play and know to interrupt it when necessary.

Dogs can get over aroused when playing with people too, and it can be harder to spot the signs of too much arousal when you're in the middle of the excitement and having fun yourself—until it has gone too far and all of a sudden the fun is over. It's not always easy to calm dogs down once they get riled up, especially when they're hanging from your elbow.[9]

It might not be you who is on the receiving end when your dog gets into trouble. We've seen too many cases of dogs who played appropriately with one person, but not others. Perhaps your field-bred Labrador Retriever gently mouths your husband's hand without a problem—but then relentlessly bites at you when you try to walk him around the neighborhood. You might have an adorable Cocker Spaniel who gently nips at your arm

---

9 See page 79 for the signs of an over aroused dog.

in play, but ends up terrifying the visiting five-year-old when he does the same to her. (Can you spell l-a-w-s-u-i-t?) Remember that the actions of both people and dogs can be initiated almost unconsciously if they are repeated often enough. (Think of your foot pressing on the brake pedal—do you have to consciously decide to move your foot off the accelerator?) If a dog has spent years closing his mouth around a person's body parts, he's going to be less inhibited about doing it in the wrong situation. The result can lead to injury and heartbreak, so take our advice and don't go there.

Start Early

If you get a puppy, it's up to you to teach your puppy not to play by biting and mouthing on hands or arms (or feet or ankles or calves or shoulders or hair or noses or. . .). A puppy's first toys are his littermates, so every young dog goes to his new home with the habit of grabbing any body part he can wrap his mouth around. You can use this to your advantage, and teach your new pup that human skin is remarkably tender and that he needs to be extra gentle with his mouth around people. This is called learning "bite inhibition."

Try yelping OUCH! or AWRP! fast and loud when a pup puts pressure on your hand or arm with his teeth. You want to startle him just enough so that he stops mouthing your hand, even for just a microsecond. The instant he does, immediately encourage your pup to play with an appropriate toy by waving it in front of his face (no closer than a foot—you don't want to scare him!) and then tossing it one or two feet away. When we say "immediately encourage him to play with an appropriate toy," we mean *immediately* (as in half a second). When your pup is in play mode, he's going to want to wrap his mouth around something (anything!), so provide an alternative target before he can get back to your wrist! Teach your dog that there are lots of toys in the world, but your body is not one of them. Get in the habit of always having a toy in your hand or pocket when you have a young pup in the house—it'll pay off in the months and years to come.

We have one last, but important reminder about puppies and play. No matter how young your pup is, he's learning how to behave around people every second that you interact, and every lesson will inform how he behaves as an adult. It might be cute (okay, it *is* cute) to have a little puppy dive into your lap and slather your face with sloppy kisses, but it's not so cute when he weighs eighty pounds and he's knocking dear old Aunt Nellie to the floor.

Of course, puppies can't be expected to have the manners of an adult dog, any more than little kids are expected to sit quietly through a three-hour opera. However, that doesn't mean that we should encourage our young dogs to behave in ways that won't be so cute once their "puppy privileges" are gone. Learn to imagine each of your pup's actions as being done by a full-size adult dog, and be very thoughtful about which behaviors you encourage and which behaviors you work to inhibit.

No Rough-and-Tumble Wrestle Play

We hereby apologize in advance to the men of the world, because this recommendation is primarily directed to them. Almost all of our clients who wrestle play with their dogs are men. It's a guy thing, no question about it. "Rough-and-tumble wrestle play" is so common in the males of some primate species that scientists in the field can use it as a way to identify the gender of their subjects. We both love guys (guys in general and our own special guys in particular), so believe us when we say we're not being sexist or critical when we recommend against wrestle play with dogs. We're just trying to keep you and your dog safe and out of trouble while you enjoy playing together.

Wrestle play is highly stimulating, and emotional arousal can get the best of any dog. Remember that many of the actions in canine play are similar to those used in serious fights or predation. A dog who misinterprets another individual's actions may feel he is only defending himself, or he may feel a need to remind another dog of what's appropriate and what's not. It's the same fundamental problem as the one that gets dogs into trouble if you let them bite at you, except during wrestle play, you are down on the ground with your face next to a predator who has the equivalent of carpet knives in his mouth.

Ponder all this when your five-year old niece starts to get down on the floor and play with your dog. And yes, it's true, there are lots of dogs who *can* wrestle play for years without a problem or who would never harm a child no matter what the child did. However, please believe us that there are lots of dogs that have been fine for years, until... We've seen far too much of that in our office, and we don't want the next case to be yours.[10]

Take Out the Teasing

Be thoughtful about teasing your dog. It's not always a bad thing to do—sometimes playing "hard to get" can stimulate a dog's interest in a toy or a game—but continuing it for too long can frustrate your dog or teach her never to trust you. It's fine to wave a tug toy momentarily out of your dog's reach, but then give her access to it once she looks interested. It can be fun to fake out your dog by pretending to throw the ball one way and tossing it the other way, but don't overdo it. You want to be sure that the game is as fun for her as it is for you.

Here's some teasing you should never do: poking, slapping, or pinching a dog, and then pulling your hand away before the dog can nip. This is a guaranteed, paid-for-in-advance ticket to trouble. One of us had a client whose Border Collie had to be rehomed because the man of the house played the "slap the face" game with the dog so often that every time anyone reached toward the dog he'd snap at their hand. Some people use face-slapping to get a dog revved up when starting to play, and while

---

10 We should mention that disagreements about how to play with the family dog are a common problem. On occasion in our offices, things have gotten so heated in discussions about play that we've been more worried about aggression within the couple than we have from their dog. It's understandable that men and woman disagree about how to play with the dog—the research is overwhelmingly clear that, in general, the sexes play differently from each other, and that's reflected in how we like to play with our dogs. All we can say is (1) we sympathize, (2) there are reasons that we make the suggestions we do, as we've explained in the text, and (3) we're glad there are marriage counselors all over the country.

it can be effective at doing that, it often elicits the kind of overly aroused play that can lead to trouble. Even worse, it teaches dogs to be excessively mouthy and snappy and often ends up with them getting into trouble with their teeth.

There's another reason to avoid this type of play, and it's a compelling one. Teasing dogs by slapping and poking at them may be fun for the person who chooses to do it ("look what I can get the dog to do!"), but we don't think it's much fun for the dog. This kind of "play" is reminiscent of a playground bully using his power to harass or frighten a weaker child, just because he can. It's not kind or friendly in any way. Teasers also might want to remember that, unlike the ninety-pound weakling on the beach, dogs have weapons in their mouths, and sometimes they use them when they get frustrated. Frustration is not an emotion known to result in a thoughtful, measured response, so don't send a dog into the emotional equivalent of road rage and then blame him for what happens.

The last kind of teasing that gets a lot of people (and dogs) in trouble is having "staring contests" or "stare fights." If you put your face down within inches of your dog's face and stare aggressively into his eyes, we guarantee you that your dog isn't thinking, "Oh boy! We're going to play a wonderful new game!" Direct stares are threats in canine society (just as they can be from people). You might be able to ameliorate the threat a bit by play bowing and using cheerful words, but why do it in the first place? In our experience, dogs are either confused by your mix of signals or assume that you are threatening them. Of course, dogs vary in how they respond. Stare straight into the eyes of some dogs and get ready to go to the emergency room. Working sheep dogs and law-enforcement dogs, for example, take that kind of direct eye contact very seriously. "Staring contests" from 300-pound rams or escaped convicts require the dogs to respond by going onto the offensive—how are they supposed to know that you are just kidding around?

Other dogs just get scared by staring contests. If you stare intently into the face of a soft, submissive dog, expect her to hide under the couch or piddle on your carpet. Who's having fun now? Of course, your dog's response also depends on the movements of your body and the context of your eye contact. We're not saying you should never look into your dog's eyes, but your dog knows the difference between friendly eye contact and an intense staring contest as well as you do. Do your dog a favor and find a safer and friendlier way to amuse yourself.

Know the Signs of Over Arousal

No matter how you play with your dog, you might have the type of dog who tends to get overly aroused when she gets excited. Just like some children, some dogs come hard-wired to spiral into a state of emotional overload in seemingly low-key situations. Other dogs, especially adolescents, haven't yet perfected their emotional thermostats, and need their owners to help them learn to keep their emotions in check. In either case, all dogs need their owners to know the signs of over arousal, and to know how and when to calm things down before they begin to spin out of control.

Begin by carefully observing your dog during regular play. Watch the way her body moves, and the way her eyes look. Listen carefully to her barks and play growls, if she's the kind of dog who vocalizes while playing. Become familiar with her normal repertoire, because dogs tend to do the same kinds of things when they get overly aroused, just more so. In general, their movements are faster, their leaps are higher, and their barks are louder. Sometimes you'll notice that their movements look less coordinated and less precise, as though they are physically spinning out of control (which they are!). If a dog has been play-growling, listen for the growls to get lower and to sound more threatening. On the other hand, listen for barks to become more rapid and, ironically, higher-pitched.

Some dogs add actions to their regular bag of tricks when they become overly aroused. Dogs who were politely playing tug or fetch might start leaping up and nipping at your arm. Be especially careful if your dog starts leaping up at you repeatedly, perhaps pushing off you with her forepaws, punching you with her muzzle, or clacking her teeth together while her head is directed toward you. These are dogs who might be losing emotional control or are becoming over aroused, and are telling you that you're going to be the target of their pent-up, uninhibited, energy. If this happens, it's time to put your inner playground monitor on duty. We'll explain how to do that in the next section!

Other signs that a dog is overly aroused include a retraction in the corners of the mouth as though the dog is panting from extreme overheating (but it's not that hot). Another good predictor of over arousal is a dog who simply can't stop doing what she's doing—you call; ask her to sit, come, or lie down; and she continues leaping or barking in an out-of-control kind of way. Fixed and rounded eyes can also be a sign that a dog is emotionally overloaded, and are another good reason to develop a precise picture of how your dog looks when playing appropriately.

There is another important behavior to watch for that is not necessarily related to arousal, but is potentially dangerous. If your dog has a closed mouth, along with a stiff and still body, she may be sending you a warning that a bite is on the way. Dogs who are playing politely will often stop for a second or two and look at you (a kind of self-imposed doggy time-out that prevents over arousal) but their bodies stay loose and relaxed and their mouths are usually open. However, if your dog stops all play, goes stiff and silent, and her eyes become hard and round while she stares directly at you, immediately try to break the mood by saying "Want your dinner?" or "Let's go for a walk!," and walk away. Your next step is to pick up the phone and call a good trainer or behaviorist.

If you are unsure if your dog's behavior is within the bounds of normal play, don't hesitate to work with an experienced trainer or behaviorist. It's not uncommon when you are first learning to read visual signals to start worrying about postures and expressions you never noticed before.

It's happens in many fields—young biology students discover that the world is awash in bacteria and begin to obsess about what's on the doorknob. Medical students memorize the symptoms of obscure diseases and begin to imagine they have come down with them. So, if a little knowledge begins to feel like a dangerous thing, go out of your way to work with someone more experienced who can help you decipher your observations.

Preventing Over Arousal—Teach Your Dog "All Done!"

It's always better to prevent problems than to try to fix them later, so be mindful about your role in your dog's emotions. Ask yourself if you or your family members are contributing factors in your dog's over arousal. Enthusiastic play in dogs is great fun to watch, so it is not surprising that people encourage their dogs to be goofy and out-of-control silly during play. That's often fine, but it's important to know the difference between "endearingly silly" and "about-to-bite-the-kids" crazy. Be thoughtful about your own actions, and monitor how much you stimulate your dog with your voice, or by making quick, darting movements around an already excited dog. Of course, if you really want to overexcite your dog and risk getting into trouble, try that rough-and-tumble wrestle play and face slapping we've talked about already!

It's remarkably easy to teach your dog an "All done" signal, and you'll find it useful in many contexts.[11] You can use anything that doesn't sound like another cue, perhaps "All done" or "Time's up." Begin by playing with your dog in your usual way—perhaps throwing a ball or playing tug. Once your dog is engaged in the game, say "All done" in a low, quiet voice and immediately change your posture. Stand up straight, turn slightly to the side and look away from your dog. Pause for a moment, keeping your body relaxed but staying quiet and disengaged. Most dogs will play along, and stand still for a moment too, waiting to see what happens next.

---

11 This is similar to the "Chill" cue that you can teach in tug games. We include it here for those who aren't playing tug, and because the importance of pauses in healthy play can't be overstated.

If that's the case, say "Go-o-od girl" in a low, quiet voice, stretching out the "go-o-o-o-o-o-d" so it takes a full second to say, and then resume play right away. Don't expect a long pause; all you want is a brief moment of calm. If you wait too long, you'll miss the moment and your dog will try to start the play session again by herself.

If she doesn't pause in response to the change in your behavior, even for half a second, turn and walk away, making it clear that the play session is over. However, most dogs will pause when you do (remember that appropriate play between dogs includes pauses by both dogs), giving you a chance to reinforce them for calming down for a moment. The most common mistake is to wait too long before either saying "Good" or reinitiating play.

You don't need to practice this over and over again in one play session— once or twice is plenty. We also end play sessions with "All done," which avoids having young, high-energy dogs leaping up into our faces or jamming tennis balls into our bellies. It helps to add a visual signal; try moving both your hands sideways like a baseball umpire signaling Safe! as you say "All done." Then disengage with commitment, and walk away. This isn't magic, but it's amazing how many dogs get the message immediately, and trot away to sniff the grass.

Remember that during training, you need to ask your dog to pause *before* she gets highly aroused. Teach her to respond when she has a chance to win and get reinforced. Once she's learned to calm down on cue, she'll be much more likely to do it when she is beginning to get more excited, but she can't learn a new skill when she's too excited to think.

What to Do if Your Dog Becomes Over Aroused

Sometimes even the best of trainers can't prevent a dog from spinning out of control. If that happens to you, your first job is to stay quiet and calm yourself. Overly excited dogs generate enough energy to power a small city—the last thing you want to do is add more to the mix. If you've worked on the cue "All done," try that first, keeping your voice low and calm. (This is easier said than done, we know.) But even if your mind is screaming "NO! NO! NO!" try to convince your mouth to speak as though you felt in complete control of the situation. (Hey, this is your chance to become an actor!) Be mindful of your body as well; move only as much as you need to and move slowly and purposefully.

You can also try asking your dog, in your most calm and confident voice, to sit. Use a clear visual signal along with your voice—visual cues tend to get more attention from dogs, especially when they are excited. If you can get your dog to sit, even for a moment, you're already ahead of the game. Your dog's posture affects her emotions, and moving into a sit helps her internal physiology settle down along with her hindquarters. (There's a reason that police usually tell people to sit down during a domestic dispute!)

If your dog sits but pops up again, that's okay; just ask for another sit. You can ask her to stay if that's a skill she's mastered, but it's okay to ask for several sits in a row, as long as you stay quiet and calm about it. Whenever she calms down in the slightest way, use that long, calming "Go-o-o-o-o-o-o-o-o-o-o-o-d" to reinforce her without getting her revved up again.

If you get no response, you might try surprising your dog with an out-of-context cue like "Wanna go on a walk?" or "Dinner Time!" Who cares that you're at the dog park and the dinner bowl is five miles away? If you can stop your dog from an emotional spiral, more power to you! If it works, reinforce the attention with a "Goooooooooood dog" or other soothing words of praise. (However, avoid praise words that themselves hype up your dog, like "Yes-Yes-Yes!!!"). You can also try simply walking away, or quietly attaching the leash to your dog's collar and striding confidently away. It's an option that professional trainers are quick to use if they feel it's necessary.

SUMMARY

There is great value in play beyond the simple, yet important, fact that it is fun. What play can do for you and your dog in terms of training, emotional control, and social bonding is nothing short of extraordinary. Play is powerful, and deserves to be a top priority for us all. Our wish is for everyone who has dogs to play with them in joyful and healthy ways, and to keep learning new ways to do so. We truly believe that this will make dogs and people alike happier, along with making our miraculous relationships with one another even stronger.

In the wise words of Ralph Waldo Emerson

"It is a happy talent to know how to play."

So off you go, with our warmest wishes… it's play time!

ACKNOWLEDGEMENTS

It takes a village (or a pack?) to write a book, and we are grateful to many people for their advice and encouragement. Ian Dunbar, Aimee Moore, and Pia Silvani have all been important sources of information and inspiration about the importance of play, and our dogs are the better for it. We are also grateful to the reviewers of the manuscript: Rick Axsom, Andrea Jennings, Aimee Moore, Denise Swedlund, Julie Vanderloop, and Chelse Wieland all gave thoughtful feedback on earlier drafts of this booklet. We are also grateful to toy expert extraordinaire, Julie Vanderloop, and to our hard-working toy testers: Bugsy, Cooper, Keanu, Lassie, Mia, Ringo, Makara, Will, and Zooey. We thank our editor, Susan Tasaki, for her skill in manuscript repair, and for doing her work in such a timely fashion. We wish everyone mentioned here, dog and human alike, could all come over and play sometime!

RESOURCES AND REFERENCES

General Training Books

Dunbar, I. 1996. *How to Teach a New Dog Old Tricks*. Berkeley, CA: James and Kenneth

King, T. 2004. *Parenting Your Dog*. Neptune, NJ: T.F.H. Publications.

McConnell, P.B. 2002. *The Other End of the Leash: Why We Do What We Do Around Dogs*. New York: Ballantine.

McConnell, P. B. and Moore, A.M. 2006. *Family Friendly Dog Training: A Six-Week Program for You and Your Dog*. Black Earth, WI: McConnell Publishing.

Miller, P. 2007. *Positive Perspectives 2: Know Your Dog, Train Your Dog*. Wenatchee, WA: Dogwise Publishing.

Silvani, P. & Eckhardt, L. 2005. *Raising Puppies and Kids Together: A Guide for Parents*. Neptune City, NJ: T.F.H. Publications.

Yin, S. 2004. *How to Behave So Your Dog Behaves*. Neptune, NJ: T.F.H. Publications.

Other Books/DVDs About Play

Bennett, R. 2007. *Off-Leash Dog Play: A Complete Guide to Safety and Fun*. Woodbridge, VA: Dream Dog Productions.

London, K.B. 2008. *Canine Play, Including Its Relationship to Aggression*. Eagle, ID: Tawzer Dog Videos.

Miller, P. 2008. *Play With Your Dog*. Wenatchee, WA: Dogwise Publishing.

Silvani, P. 2008. *Playtime: The Good, The Bad, The Ugly*. Eagle, ID: Tawzer Dog Videos.

Trick Training Books

Bielakiewicz, G &. Bielakiewicz, P. 2005. *The Only Dog Tricks Book You'll Ever Need.* Cincinnati, OH: Adams Media.

Sundance, K. & Chalcy. 2007. *101 Dog Tricks: Step-by-Step Activities to Engage, Challenge, and Bond with Your Dog.* Beverly, MA: Quarry Books.

Hunter, R. 1996. *Fun Nosework for Dogs.* Franklin, NY: Howln Moon Press.

Dainty, S. 2007. *50 Games to Play with Your Dog.* Neptune City, NJ: T.F.H. Publications.

Research on Play and Social Relationships

Bekoff, M. & Byers, J. A. 1981. A critical reanalysis of the ontogeny of mammalian social and locomotor play: An ethological hornet's nest. In Immelmann K., Barlow G. W., Petrinovich L., & Main M. (Eds.) *Behavioral development: The Bielefeld interdisciplinary project.* (pp. 296-337). New York: Cambridge University Press.

Bekoff, M. & Byers, J. A. 1998. *Animal Play: Evolutionary, Comparative, and Ecological Perspectives.* Cambridge: Cambridge University Press.

Burkhardt, G. M. 2005. *The Genesis of Animal Play: Testing the Limits.* Cambridge, MA: MIT Press.

Fagen, R. 1981. *Animal Play Behavior.* New York: Oxford University Press.

Koda, N. 2001. *Development of play behavior between potential guide dogs for the blind and human raisers.* Behavioural Processes 53: 41-46.

Miklósi, A. 2008. *Dog Behaviour, Evolution, and Cognition.* Oxford, UK.Oxford University Press.

Prato-Previde, E., Fallani, G., & Valsecchi, P. 2006. Gender differences in owners interacting with pet dogs: An observational study. *Ethology* 112: 64-73.

Rooney, N. J., Bradshaw, J. W. S., & Robinson, I. H. 2001. Do dogs respond to play signals given by humans? *Animal Behaviour* 61: 715-722.

Rooney, N. J. & Bradshaw, J. W. S. 2002. An experimental study of the effects of play upon the dog-human relationship. *Applied Animal Behaviour Science* 75: 161-176.

Rooney, N. J. & Bradshaw, J. W. S. 2003. Links between play and dominance and attachment dimensions of dog-human relationships. *Journal of Applied Animal Welfare Science* 6: 67-94.

Spinka, M., Newberry, R. C., & Bekoff M. 2001. Mammalian play: Training for the unexpected. *The Quarterly Review of Biology* 76: 141-168.

Topál, J., Miklósi, Á., Csányi, V., & Dóka, A. 1998. Attachment behavior in dogs (Canis familiaris): a new application of Ainsworth's (1969) strange situation test. *Journal of Comparative Psychology.* 112: 219-229.

Wilson, E. O. 1975. *Sociobiology: The New Synthesis.* Cambridge, MA: Harvard University Press.

Other Books by McConnell & London

Way to Go!
  How to Housetrain a Dog of Any Age

Feisty Fido
  Help for the Leash Aggressive Dog

Feeling Outnumbered?
  How to Manage and Enjoy Your Multi-dog Household

Other Books by Patricia McConnell

The Other End of the Leash
  Why We Do What We Do Around Dogs

For the Love of a Dog
  Understanding Emotion in You and Your Best Friend

Tales of Two Species:
  Essays on Loving and Living with Dogs

Family Friendly Dog Training
  Six-Week Program for You and Your Dog

Puppy Primer

How to be Leader of the Pack and have your dog love you for it!

The Cautious Canine:
  How to Help Dogs Conquer Their Fears

I'll Be Home Soon!
  How to Prevent and Treat Separation Anxiety

The Fastidious Feline
  How to Prevent and Treat Litter Box Problems

All books, booklets (and many DVDs) are available at
www.patriciamcconnell.com

Karen B. London, Ph.D., is an Ethologist, a Certified Applied Animal Behaviorist and a Certified Pet Dog Trainer whose clinical work focuses on the evaluation and treatment of serious behavioral problems in dogs. Her research and scholarly publications cover such diverse topics as interactions between species that live together, defensive and aggressive behavior, evolution of social behavior, communication within and between species, learning, and parental investment. Karen London is currently a columnist and blogger for *The Bark* magazine and served for three years on the Animal Behavior Society's Board of Professional Certification. She has written widely about training and behavior as well as given educational seminars and speeches on canine behavior for trainers, veterinary and shelter staff, and the public. She is a lecturer at Northern Arizona University for a tropical biology field course to Nicaragua, and has given guest lectures in Animal Behavior at several universities. She lives in Flagstaff, Arizona, with her husband and their two young sons.

Patricia B. McConnell, Ph.D. is an Ethologist and Certified Applied Animal Behaviorist who has consulted with cat and dog lovers for over twenty years. She combines a thorough understanding of the science of behavior with years of practical, applied experience. Her nationally syndicated radio show, Wisconsin Public Radio's *Calling All Pets*, played in over 115 cities for 14 years. She is the behavior columnist for the *The Bark* magazine ("the New Yorker of Dog Magazines") and a Consulting Editor for the Journal of Comparative Psychology. She is Adjunct Associate Professor in Zoology at the University of Wisconsin-Madison, teaching "The Biology and Philosophy of Human/Animal Relationships." Dr. McConnell is a much sought after speaker and seminar presenter, speaking to training organizations, veterinary conferences, academic meetings and animal shelters around the world about dog and cat behavior, and on science-based and humane solutions to serious behavioral problems. She is the author of nine books on training and behavioral problems, as well as the critically acclaimed books *The Other End of the Leash: Why We Do What We Do Around Dogs* and *For the Love of a Dog: Understanding Emotion in You and Your Best Friend.*